100

THE ROUGH GUIDE TO THE
BEST PLACES
IN IRELAND

100

THE ROUGH GUIDE TO THE
BEST PLACES
IN IRELAND

DISTRIBUTION

UK, Ireland and Europe
Apa Publications (UK) Ltd; sales@roughguides.com

United States and Canada
Ingram Publisher Services; ips@ingramcontent.com

Australia and New Zealand
Booktopia; retailer@booktopia.com.au

Worldwide
Apa Publications (UK) Ltd; sales@roughguides.com

SPECIAL SALES, CONTENT LICENSING AND CO-PUBLISHING

Rough Guides can be purchased in bulk quantities at discounted prices. We can create special editions, personalized jackets and corporate imprints tailored to your needs. Email: sales@roughguides.com
roughguides.com

Printed in China

HELP US UPDATE

We've gone to a lot of effort to ensure that this first edition of The Rough Guide to the 100 Best Places in Ireland is accurate and up-to-date. But if you feel we've got it wrong or left something out, we'd like to know.
Please send your comments with the subject line "Rough Guides 100 Best Places in Ireland" to mail@uk.roughguides.com. We'll credit all contributions and send a copy of the next edition (or any other Rough Guide if you prefer) for the very best emails.

THE ROUGH GUIDE TO THE
100 BEST PLACES IN IRELAND

Editor: Kate Drynan
Commissioned by: Kate Drynan
Picture Editor: Tom Smyth
Designer: Pradeep Thapliyal
Head of DTP and Pre-press: Rebeka Davies
Head of Publishing: Sarah Clark

100

THE ROUGH GUIDE TO THE BEST PLACES IN IRELAND

INTRODUCTION

Ireland's appeal lies in its raw beauty. An island split politically in two, its history may be turbulent, but its beauty and warm welcome are a constant whether you go north or south. A country said to display all forty shades of green, Ireland's rolling interior is infinitely lush, dotted with woodland and farmland, low-lying mountains, lakes and pretty river valleys. Its coastal route is surrounded on all sides by the deep, bracing blue waters of the Atlantic Ocean, peppered with craggy outcrops, offshore inhabited islands that are a step back in time and long sandy beaches that can rival any of those in the Caribbean.

Its cosmopolitan capital Dublin may be small but there is plenty to enjoy in its museums and art galleries and fine Georgian architecture, while burgeoning Belfast has emerged as a city with plenty of draw, from its age-old saloons, opera house and fascinating Titanic Quarter. And up and down the divide you'll discover medieval cities, Viking towns, moon-like landscapes, bogland and breathtakingly beautiful loughs, castles, gardens and demesnes, some seemingly undiscovered but many forever idolised in the paintings and prose of the country's many famed artists, poets and literary heroes.

Ireland is a place in which to slow down and take it all in. At times because the landscape simply demands it, with many a winding, narrow road; and at others because you must match the pace of its people, as unhurried as the sheep or cattle that stop traffic along its quiet country lanes. Thirty-two counties to explore, each with a very special and distinctive appeal.

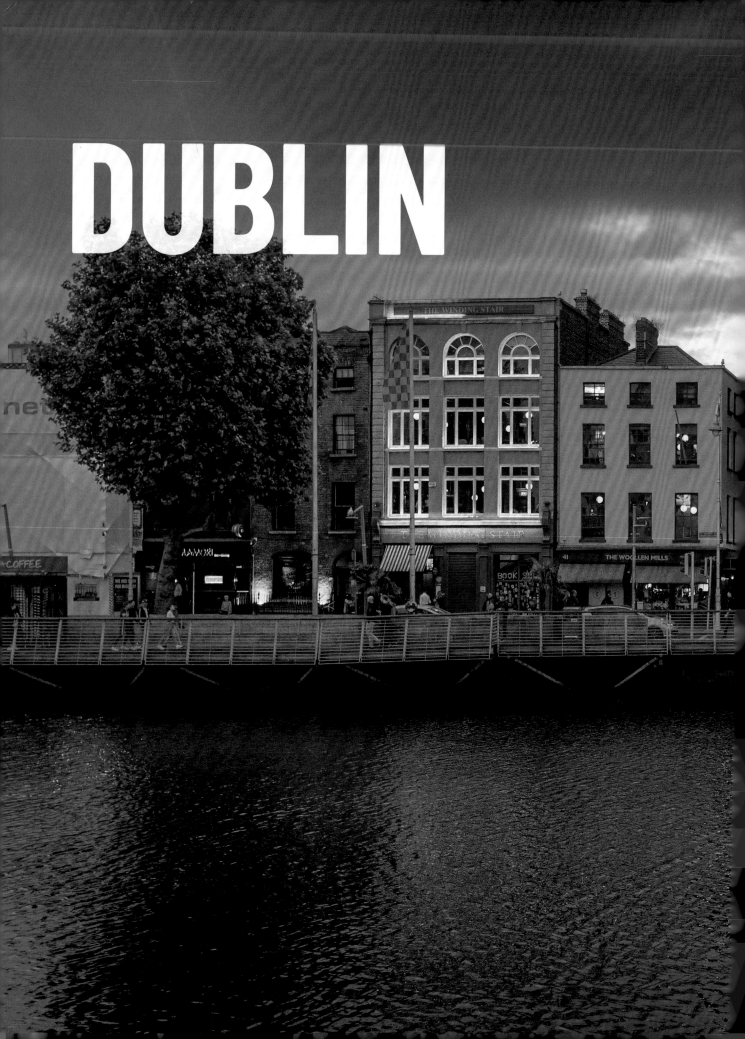

The cobblestoned entrance to the brewery

GUINNESS STOREHOUSE

It goes without saying that no visit to Dublin, or indeed Ireland, is complete without a pint or two of the black stuff. But better than that, go and see how it is produced. The Guinness Storehouse is a seven-storey building built around a soaring glass atrium in the shape of a pint of beer – which would contain 14.3 million pints if full. It's located on the main road out of the city, in between the Irish Museum of Modern Art and St Patrick's Cathedral. The building pays homage to the history of the perennially popular stout, from its founding in 1759 when Arthur Guinness began brewing on the site, through to the brewing process itself and an exhibition on the company's legendary marketing campaigns – the Guinness White Horses advert, anyone? Naturally, there are plenty of opportunities to sup a pint during your visit, in particular up on the rooftop *Gravity Bar*, where a free pint is included as part of the admission. Hell, why stop there? Kick back with another whilst observing the comings and goings on the streets below or stay for lunch. And whilst you don't necessarily have to be a fan of the tipple to make this a worthwhile trip, it certainly helps.

The glass-fronted *Gravity Bar* atop the seven-storey building

Guinness and seafood at the *1837 Bar*

Guinness is known for its great advertising

The brewing process explained in the on-site exhibition

13

Man in Bloomsday costume at the James Joyce Centre

Painter at *Davy Byrnes*, Bloomsday

James Joyce statue, North Earl Street

James Joyce Tower and Museum, Sandycove

JAMES JOYCE PILGRIMAGE

It's not too far-fetched to suggest that it was *Ulysses* – the modernist master-piece by the Irish author James Joyce and a book referred to by TS Eliot as "one to which we are all indebted, and from which none of us can escape" – that really put Dublin on the international map. And it is why so many Joyce aficionados make the pilgrimage to the birthplace of the literary titan. Start at the statue of the great man on North Earl Street before taking in the James Joyce Centre and then head across the river towards St Stephen's Green and the Museum of Literature Ireland, both the centre and museum are full to bursting with Joycean treasures. Hunt down, too, the fourteen brass plaques laid in pavements around the city which mark out the walk taken by the novel's chief protagonist Leopold Bloom during the course of the day. Further afield, seek out Clifton School in Dalkey where Joyce once taught history, and the engrossing James Joyce Tower and Museum in Sandycove, which holds one of two official death masks – the other is in Zurich where he died, and was buried, in 1941. The big one is Bloomsday on June 16 – the fictional date on which the novel's events took place, in 1904 – when the fair city is awash with Joycean jollity, courtesy of readings, talks, re-enactments, singing, food, fancy dress (boater hats at the ready), and tonnes more literary lunacy.

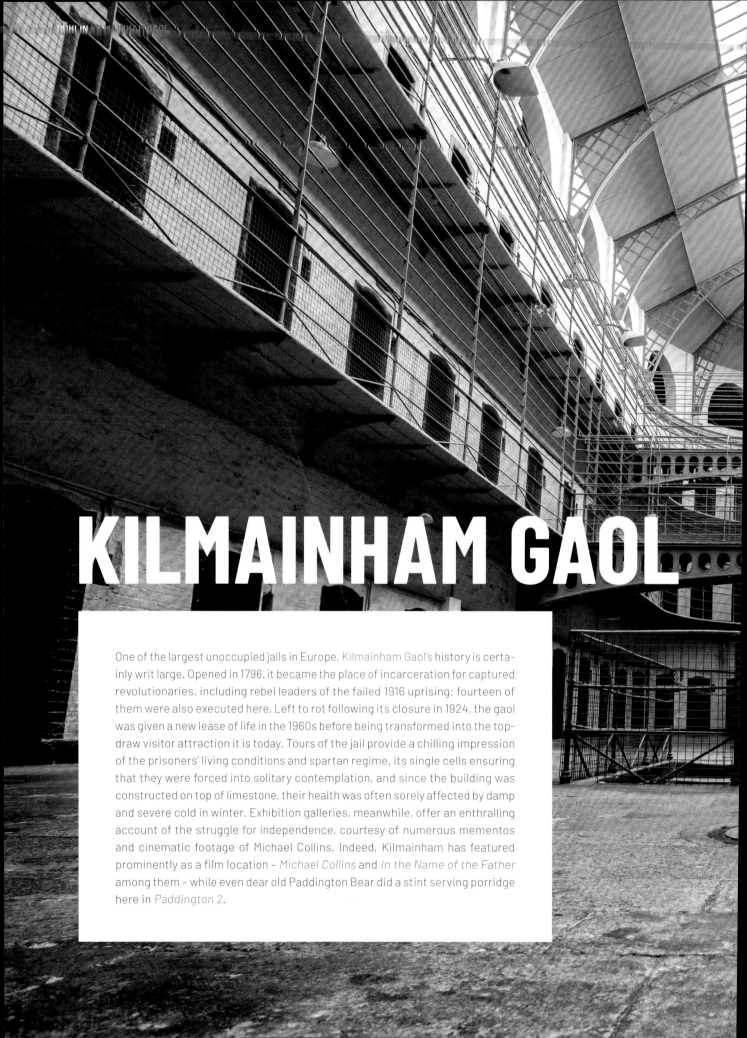

KILMAINHAM GAOL

One of the largest unoccupied jails in Europe, Kilmainham Gaol's history is certainly writ large. Opened in 1796, it became the place of incarceration for captured revolutionaries, including rebel leaders of the failed 1916 uprising; fourteen of them were also executed here. Left to rot following its closure in 1924, the gaol was given a new lease of life in the 1960s before being transformed into the top-draw visitor attraction it is today. Tours of the jail provide a chilling impression of the prisoners' living conditions and spartan regime, its single cells ensuring that they were forced into solitary contemplation, and since the building was constructed on top of limestone, their health was often sorely affected by damp and severe cold in winter. Exhibition galleries, meanwhile, offer an enthralling account of the struggle for independence, courtesy of numerous mementos and cinematic footage of Michael Collins. Indeed, Kilmainham has featured prominently as a film location – *Michael Collins* and *In the Name of the Father* among them – while even dear old Paddington Bear did a stint serving porridge here in *Paddington 2*.

The historic jail

NATIONAL GALLERY OF IRELAND

Ireland's foremost gallery is a sprawling institution housing the best of the nation's art, including the National Portrait Collection, as well as a dazzling spread of European masterpieces and rotating contemporary exhibitions. Don't forget to pick up a map before you dive in looking for gems, with four massive wings to explore. Highlights include Caravaggio's *The Taking of Christ* (hidden away for over half a century in a house just a mile away from the gallery), a number of works from Rembrandt, Monet and their contemporaries, fine paintings by Spanish artists from Goya to Picasso, and much more besides. In-depth guided tours are an ideal way to explore this treasure trove. Time it right and you'll be able to see *Hellelil and Hildebrand, the Meeting on the Turret Stairs* by Frederic William Burton, unveiled only for an hour on Thursday and Sunday afternoons to protect its delicate watercolours from light exposure. Sculpture, photography and furniture all feature alongside paintings, drawings and prints in this expansive gallery, as well as a complete Irish art library and comprehensive digital archive collections. There's also a bookshop and café to keep you on your feet along with a host of other Dublin landmarks just moments away.

Inside the gallery

The Grand Gallery is lined with great art

The imposing exterior

Appreciating fine art

Howth Head

Baily Lighthouse marks the southeast point of Howth

Colourful heather in season

Shane's Howth Adventures Safari Hiking Tour

Shane's Howth Adventures Coastal Walking tour

HOWTH CLIFF WALK

Clinging to the slopes of a rocky peninsula and overlooking an animated fishing harbour, the village of Howth (rhymes with 'both'), at the end of the DART line has a wonderful Cliff Walk. The route takes in great views south over the city to the Wicklow Mountains and north to the Boyne Valley. The footpath runs for some 8km clockwise from the village round to the west-facing side of the peninsula, followed by a 3km walk by the sea along Strand Road and Greenfield Road to Sutton DART station; allow at least three hours. You first head east out of Howth village along Balscadden Road to the Nose of Howth, before the path turns south, crossing the slopes above the cliffs, which are covered in colourful gorse and bell heather in season; the area known as The Summit. Just inland of the path, has a pub and a café. The southeast point is marked by the Baily Lighthouse. The path along the south-facing coast of the peninsula is the most spectacular part of the walk, offering sublime views of cliffs, secluded beaches and rocky islands.

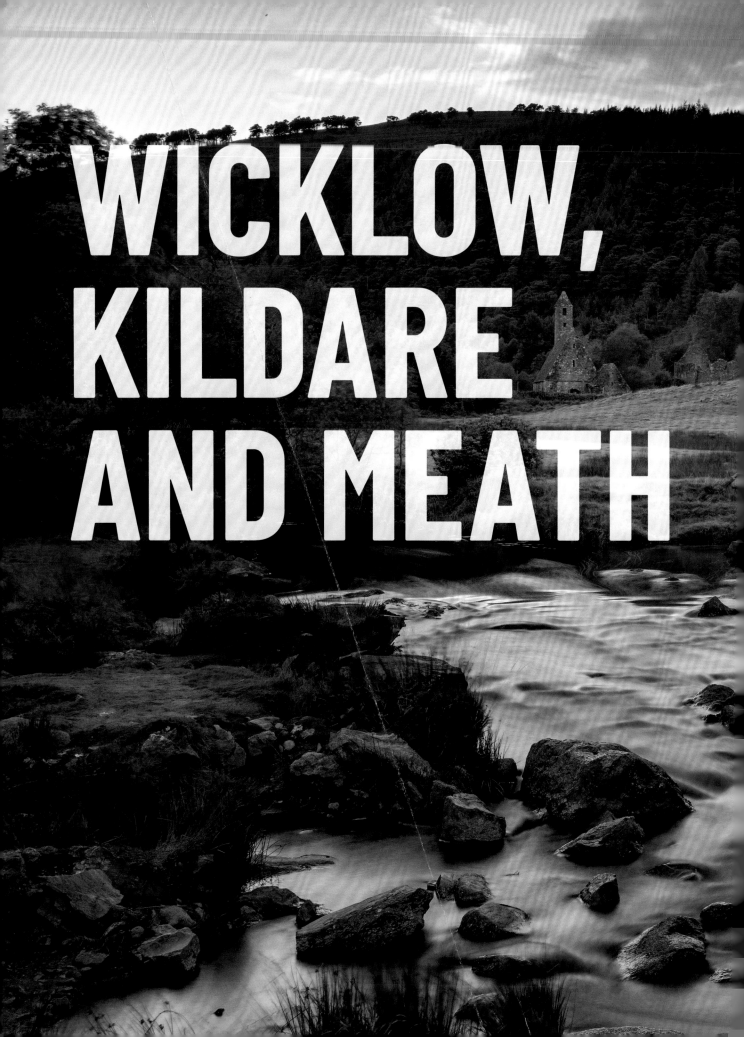

WICKLOW, KILDARE AND MEATH

Aerial view of Avondale House and the Treetop Walk

Avonmore River

Fun for all ages high in the canopies

The lofty Viewing Tower

AVONDALE FOREST PARK

Avondale is a multi-sensory joy: listen to the sweetest birdsong and the gentle rustle of leaves; feel the breeze dance across your shoulders; and experience a rush of adrenaline as the forest floor disappears beneath your feet. Take delight in interactive, educational displays and dart across lofty bridges marked by bursts of brightly painted flowers. As you gently ascend into the canopies of the trees, the beauty of nature is literally all around you. Trace the looping pathway of the Treetop Walk before climbing the spiralling Viewing Tower to its dizzying summit: a 124ft-high lookout platform. Once there, stop to soak in the exceptional viewpoints north, south, east and west, before the final adrenalin kick – a super slide that will rocket you back down to earth, and fast. Back on firm ground, giddy from the thrill, regain your composure with a browse in the giftshop or wander over to the café with its playground and pretty courtyard garden. For those with a zest for more, hours of walking is possible on the five hundred-acre grounds of the Forest Park, while history buffs might enjoy a visit to Avondale House. Those keen to experience it all over again needn't fear, Avondale's treetop magic will call you back again.

MOUNT USHER

Designed by Dubliner Edward Walpole in 1868, in the Robinsonian style made famous by the eponymous gardener, Mount Usher Gardens shelter a plethora of rare trees, shrubs and flowers, including dazzling rhododendrons, azaleas and maples, and the finest eucalyptus specimens in Europe. It's all growing in an informal style in its woodlands and meadows in Ashford, County Wicklow, just 35 minutes outside of Dublin city centre and serviced by bus number 133. Running through the gardens is the River Vartry, broken up here by a remarkable series of nineteenth-century weirs, watercourses and suspension bridges. The Avoca café on site will ensure you remain well fed and refreshed while the Courtyard Shops are a tempting diversion. Come on a sunny day and delight in one of the country's finest gardens.

A river runs through it...

River Vartry weir

Riverside pathways

Suspension bridges cross the river throughout the gardens

The Upper Lake and loop walking trail

Glendalough Graveyard

St Kevin's Church

The Upper Lake on a clear day

GLENDALOUGH

A deep glaciated valley in the heart of the Wicklow Mountains, Glendalough (valley of the two lakes) provides a delightfully atmospheric location for some of the best-preserved monastic sites in Ireland and some lovely, marked walking trails. Despite the coach hordes, enough of the valley's tranquillity remains for you to understand what drew monks and pilgrims here. The Glendalough Visitor Centre, car park and the main monastic site are on the eastern side of the Lower Lake, while further west up the valley is the more impressive Upper Lake, with its wooded cliffs and dramatic waterfall. You can drive to the Upper Lake along the north side of the valley, but it's more enjoyable to walk from the Deer Stone along the signposted Green Road (part of the Wicklow Way), a scenic track that skirts the south side of the Lower Lake. After twenty minutes or so, this will bring you to the Upper Lake and the tiny, ruined, late tenth century, Romanesque Reefert Church, whose cemetery is said to contain the graves of local chieftains. From here a path runs up to St Kevin's Cell, the remains of a beehive hut on a promontory overlooking the lake. One of Glendalough's most famous monuments, the 30m-high Round Tower is nestled in a valley close to the Lower Lake. For superb views of both lakes and a demanding hike, follow The Spinc, a looping trail of 9.5km that'll take close to four hours.

The Round Tower, Glendalough

HUNTINGBROOK

Jimi Blake, the owner and creator of Huntingbrook Gardens, began the transformation of twenty acres of a County Wicklow woodland valley in 2001. He has developed it into a highly regarded and internationally renowned garden full of inspiring and unusual plant combinations, divided into five areas each with its own style and atmosphere. Ashley's Garden showcases Jimi's famous exotic planting, with many species having been brought back from trips to China. Colours are vibrant and opulent, and this garden really shines in summer. Fred's Garden shows off contrasting textures, while the Sand Garden, the most recent project, features hundreds of succulents and cacti. The Woodland Garden is wonderfully sheltered by deciduous and coniferous trees, with beds full of shade-loving woodland plants, and boasts huge collections of various snowdrops and epimediums. Finally, The Valley is both stunning and peaceful, with views over the Wicklow Mountains and glimpses of a ring fort and standing stones. Planting includes collections of rhododendrons, acers and magnolias. Jimi's style is unconventional and the gardens are everchanging as a result of experimentation, sometimes with plants no one would expect to survive in Ireland. A must-see for any plant lover, providing endless inspiration and pushing boundaries.

A dazzling summer display

Breakfast in the Green Barn

Bacon and egg with hollandaise sauce

The gardens

Burtown House

Seasonal asparagus with a poached egg

THE GREEN BARN BURTOWN HOUSE

Looking for a bite of the best breakfast in Ireland? This is just where to find it. The inviting, light-drenched *The Green Barn* in Burtown House in County Kildare with its high-beamed ceiling, floor-to-ceiling windows, chunky wooden tables and wonderful lanterns is the perfect spot to enjoy a leisurely brunch in style. The walls are peppered with pretty prints for sale and mirrors and plants and stylish decorative pieces sit pleasingly everywhere you cast your eye. Be seated at your table by one of the friendly staff and enjoy a pot of tea or coffee and a freshly squeezed juice alongside some granola or a cooked breakfast

such as pancakes with berries or bacon and maple syrup. Or opt for the innovative take on the full Irish, with kale and seasonal greens on a muffin topped with sausages and streaky bacon alongside a feta and scallion potato cake, the lot drizzled with home-made hollandaise and served with a side of sourdough toast. Sit back and enjoy the view of the landscaped gardens and don't be in a rush for lunch. On a sunny day, it's simply superb.

NATIONAL STUD

It's no secret that the Irish profess a deep-rooted attachment to all things equine, something that's very much in evidence at the Irish National Stud on the Curragh in Kildare, an hour or so southwest of Dublin. The stud was established in 1900 by Colonel William Hall Walker, of Scotch whisky fame, whose methods were as eccentric as they were successful: each newborn foal's horoscope was read, and those on whom the stars didn't shine were sold, regardless of their lineage or physical characteristics. Presented to the British government in 1915 – henceforth known as the British National Stud – it was finally transferred to the Irish government in 1944. There's a day's worth of entertainment here, from tours of the stud and a visit to the Irish Racehorse Experience – where you get the opportunity to own, train and race your own thoroughbred, as well as have a go at some commentary, to a stroll around the fabled Japanese Gardens. But the stars, of course, are the horses themselves. The Living Legends field is home to many retired prize horses; indeed, many a great racehorse has been raised here, among them the 2009 Derby winner, *Sea the Stars*. From February until July, you should be able to see mares and their young foals in the paddocks.

Million-euro horses at the Irish National Stud

The Irish Racehorse Experience

The Japanese Gardens

Castletown House

The opulent drawing room

A Venetian chandelier inside the house

The Wonderful Barn

CASTLETOWN HOUSE

Castletown House is a beautiful Palladian mansion in County Kildare, considered to be the finest example of the style in Ireland. Extensive restoration had to be carried out on the building after it was left vacant and vandalised in the 1960s, and it became the flagship project of the Irish Georgian Society. Most of its contents having been sold off, also in the '60s, extraordinary efforts have been made in subsequent years to buy back furniture, paintings and other decorative items which are now on display for public appreciation. However, the curiosity of the Wonderful Barn on the edge of the estate may be considered by some to be the main attraction. Certainly not what you expect to find when looking for a 'barn', this corkscrew-shaped building has baffled visitors, and the reason for its unusual construction is still something of a mystery. The generally accepted view is that was built as a store for grain, and to provide employment to local people following the famine of the 1740s. Unfortunately, it is not possible to enter the building but the view of it alone is worth the trip. It can also be seen from within Castletown House.

Newgrange

Stone carvings

Winter solstice sunrise

View from inside

NEWGRANGE

Newgrange is unquestionably the most striking of the *Brú na Bóinne* mounds, not least because its facade of white quartz stones and round granite boulders has been reassembled. The quartz originally came from Wicklow, the granite from the Mourne and Carlingford areas, exemplifying the mind-boggling levels of resources and organisation lavished on this project, by these farmers who used nothing but simple tools of wood and stone. It has been estimated that the tumulus, which is over 75m in diameter, weighs 200,000 tons in total and would have taken around forty years to build. It was the final resting place of a high-status family within the Neolithic community – the cremated remains and grave goods of at least five people were recovered from the burial chamber during excavation – but seems also to have had a wider purpose as a ritual site or gathering place. The entrance stone is one of the finest examples of the art of the tomb-builders, who carved spectacular but enigmatic spirals, chevrons, lozenges and other geometric designs onto many of the large stones around the mound and up the 19m passage. The tomb's pivotal feature, however, is a roof-box above the entrance whose slit was perfectly positioned to receive the first rays of the rising sun on the day of the winter solstice (December 21); the light first peeps into the cruciform burial chamber itself before spreading its rays along the length of the passage.

Winter solstice inside the chamber

The castle illuminated after dark

TRIM CASTLE

War raged in Ireland for many centuries of its long and distinguished history, reflected in the roughly 30,000 castles and fortifications that stud the land. These are not the ostentatious, show castles of royals and gentry as found in England and the rest of Europe, but fortified seats and outposts built by chieftains or invaders. County Meath's Trim Castle is the mightiest fortress in Ireland, standing or otherwise, stretching over 30sq km. The largest Anglo-Norman castle ruin in Europe, it took thirty years to construct under Hugh de Lacy and his inheritors in the twelfth and thirteenth centuries. From an impregnable fortress against the Celts it grew in the following centuries, becoming a mint for currency in the fifteenth century and meeting point for parliament before eventually falling to Cromwell's occupation in 1649. Walking through its gates and along its ramparts, you might recognise its modern use as a filming location during the siege of King John's castle in *Braveheart* starring Mel Gibson. It's free to enter the grounds but with a guided tour of the whole keep costing €5, we can't see much reason to hold back. Less than an hour from Dublin, it makes for a perfect addition to a weekend away in the capital or the staging point for a foray into the country's interior.

Kayaking on the Boyne beside the castle

Sheep Gate

The Keep

Internal stairway

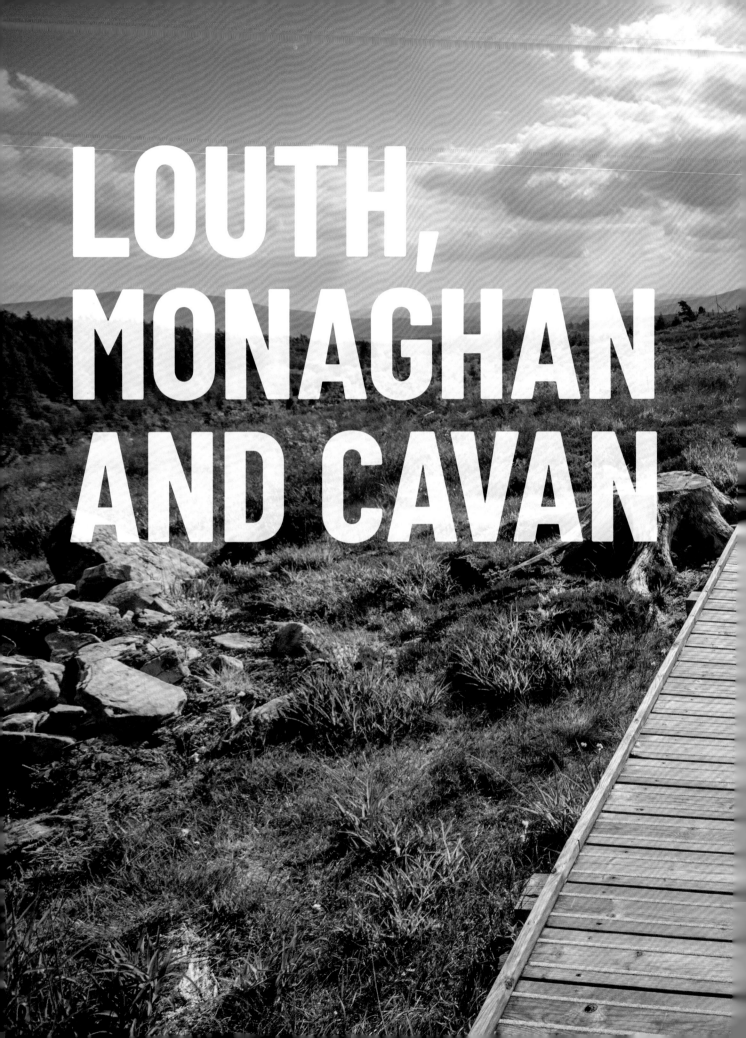

LOUTH, MONAGHAN AND CAVAN

Dramatic views of the peninsula

COOLEY PENINSULA

Separated from the north of Ireland only by Carlingford Lough, the largely off--the-radar Cooley Peninsula is a rounded 15km plug of Irish turf and granite, a beautiful and dramatic landscape bearing green-shouldered hills crested with crags and gently sloping valleys. Cooley's main settlement is colourful Carlingford, erstwhile Viking settlement but now all fifteenth-century walls and fortified townhouses, narrow cobbled streets and white-stone cotta-ges – but above all, it seems, an endless succession of quintessential Irish boozers. The peninsula is also home to what is arguably the definitive Irish legend, that of the *Táin Bó Cuailnge* (Cattle Raid of Cooley), an epic pagan odyssey of greed and self-sacrifice set around 500BC. The saga has lent its name to the 40km-long Táin Way, a circular route around Slieve Foye (587m), and up to the west above Carlingford – reckon on two days. More doable is the Greenway, which skims the lough all the way to Omeath, some 7km distant; with hilly fields on one side and the water – turquoise on a sunny day – almost emerald on another, this is a terrific outing, be it on foot or by bike.

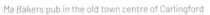
Ma Bakers pub in the old town centre of Carlingford

Carlingford Lough ferry

Carlingford town

Hiking the Cooley Peninsula

THE JUMPING CHURCH

Ireland is hardly devoid of outlandish tourist attractions, and folklore comes as standard wherever you go, but few places elicit as much intrigue as The Jumping Church in Kildemock, just south of the town of Ardlee in central County Louth. The mystery swirling around Millockstown Church (as it's formally known) revolves around how the western wall mysteriously 'jumped' to land some 3ft within the building's own foundations – hence the nickname 'Jumping Wall'. All manner of dubious theories have been posited, among them that the wall leapt inwards to exclude an unworthy corpse from the holy ground of the church interior, while another supposes that a violent storm caused the west gable of the building to move eastwards, leaving it standing in its improbable new position within the ediface. Spooky goings-on aside, this is a wonderfully tranquil spot, the church positioned atop a hill with the Carlingford and Mourne mountains (see page 223) providing a suitably ethereal backdrop.

The remains of the jumping wall

Aerial view of the estate

Gorgeous surroundings at every turn

One of the sumptuous bedrooms

A cosy fire is perfect on a cold winter's day

CASTLE LESLIE ESTATE

Fancy a spot of fishing or falconry, some horse riding, a carriage ride or perhaps a seaweed peat bath followed by a scrumptious meal and a positively perfect night's kip? Then *Castle Leslie Estate*, set on a thousand acres of County Monaghan countryside in the neat little village of Glaslough, ticks all those boxes. An almost unaltered Victorian playground built in 1871 for Sir John Leslie, 1st baronet, Castle Leslie Estate – which is still home to the founding family – is pure Gothic fantasy, fashioned in Scottish baronial style, all spiky turrets, marbled fireplaces and an extravagant library that, according to the author Jonathan Swift (one of the castle's many esteemed guests), possessed "rows of books upon its shelves, written by Leslies all about themselves".

Stay in either The Castle proper – with its flamboyantly decorated rooms chock-full of antiques and heirlooms – or The Lodge, which offers more contemporaneous touches; for families, the Old Stables Mews conversion is just the ticket. Dining-wise, take your pick from the award-winning *Snaffles Restaurant* or enjoy a more relaxed style 'pub grub' in *Conor's Bar & Lounge*, both at The Lodge. They even serve a whoppingly fab Afternoon Tea. Whatever your bed or table of choice, one thing is guaranteed: you'll have little urge to leave whatsoever.

Ready for flight

Inniskeen Round Tower

Monaghan is known as 'Kavanagh Country'

Inniskeen River Walk

Patrick Kavanagh's grave

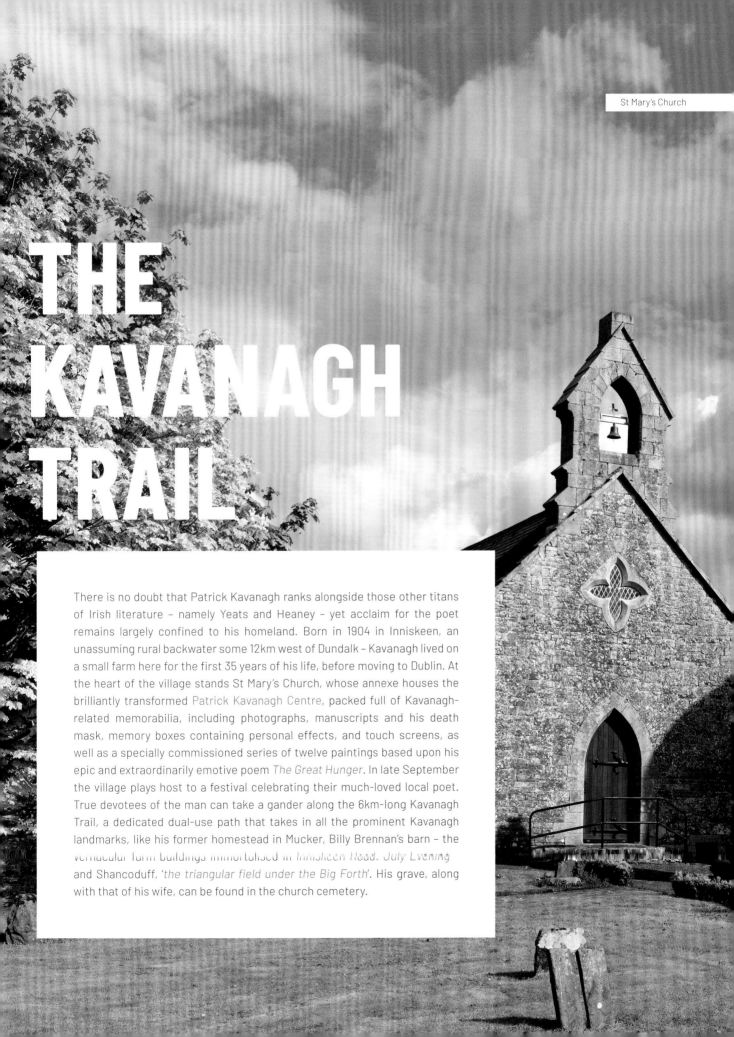

THE KAVANAGH TRAIL

There is no doubt that Patrick Kavanagh ranks alongside those other titans of Irish literature – namely Yeats and Heaney – yet acclaim for the poet remains largely confined to his homeland. Born in 1904 in Inniskeen, an unassuming rural backwater some 12km west of Dundalk – Kavanagh lived on a small farm here for the first 35 years of his life, before moving to Dublin. At the heart of the village stands St Mary's Church, whose annexe houses the brilliantly transformed Patrick Kavanagh Centre, packed full of Kavanagh-related memorabilia, including photographs, manuscripts and his death mask, memory boxes containing personal effects, and touch screens, as well as a specially commissioned series of twelve paintings based upon his epic and extraordinarily emotive poem *The Great Hunger*. In late September the village plays host to a festival celebrating their much-loved local poet. True devotees of the man can take a gander along the 6km-long Kavanagh Trail, a dedicated dual-use path that takes in all the prominent Kavanagh landmarks, like his former homestead in Mucker, Billy Brennan's barn – the vernacular farm buildings immortalised in *Inniskeen Road: July Evening* and Shancoduff, '*the triangular field under the Big Forth*'. His grave, along with that of his wife, can be found in the church cemetery.

The luxury cabin interiors

Many of the private decks overlook the lake

The hot tubs are a special treat after an active day

A typical cabin interior

The cabins

CABÜ BY THE LAKES

Cabü by the Lakes is a serene lakeside getaway in County Cavan. Individual cabins have a touch of luxe and are nestled in the midst of majestic trees, their leaves rustling softly in the breeze from dawn, pretty lanterns hanging from branches illuminate the pathways from dusk. Awake to the sound of birdsong and perhaps a chaffinch or two nesting on your private deck before grabbing a fresh coffee or pastry from the shop or rustle up a leisurely breakfast in the well-equipped kitchen. Then take to the lakes, by boat, paddleboard or kayak, or perhaps a swim in fine weather. It's car-free so gloriously quiet and there's fishing and tranquil cycle trails in the adjoining Killykeen Forest Park. The vast natural park is crisscrossed with hiking and biking trails, suitable for the whole family, with breathtaking scenery and pit-stop trucks and a home-style café to grab a coffee or cake along the way. Add to this the luxury amenities, including a Japanese bath, outdoor hot tubs and sauna, and The Sitooterie, a fire-warmed outdoor relaxation area where the children can toast marshmallows while you sip a drink from the bar, and it's easy to see why Cabü is such a restorative getaway.

Beautiful walking trails

CAVAN BURREN PARK

A vast, wind-whipped limestone plateau the Cavan Burren Park is loaded with one of Ireland's greatest troves of prehistoric treasures – megalithic tombs, cist graves and ancient stone huts – yet it's one of the least known parts of the country. Tucked away well off the tourist trail on the border between north and south, the Cavan Burren Park is a wild, desolately beautiful spot. One monument, the Giant's Grave, is nearly 8m-long and composed of one-tonne slabs arranged to align with the setting sun. Another, the Calf House, is a tomb the size of a garden shed, complete with a great hulk of stone slumped at 45 degrees; the original tomb dates back to around 4000BC but at some point a local farmer saw fit to build a wall into it, converting it into a calf shelter. A basic but informative open-air visitor centre helps make sense of this otherworldly landscape, and is also the starting point for a series of short, looped walks through the park, ranging in length from 1.3km to 3km, the shortest of which is wheelchair accessible.

The Calf House

The visitor centre

Wildflowers bordering one of the walking trails

Trail through the park

Seafood plates

Neven's mastery

A table for two

Guests can opt to stay over in *MacNean House*

MACNEAN HOUSE & RESTAURANT

It's fair to say that you'd struggle to locate *MacNean House & Restaurant* on a map, but for its many devotees, it's the centre of Ireland's foodie-verse. Secreted away in the tiny village of Blacklion on the County Cavan-Fermanagh border, the original MacNean's restaurant opened in 1969, but it wasn't until husband-and-wife team Neven and Amelda Maguire took over the reins in 2001 that its reputation began to soar. Quartered within a smart townhouse, MacNean House is one of the motherships of the modern Irish culinary revolution and now among the most sought-after experiences in the country – reckon on booking up to at least six months in advance. Expect outlandishly scintillating combinations like crispy goat's cheese with heirloom mushrooms and smoked tomato jam, monkfish with lemon fregola and buttered lobster, and buttermilk panna cotta with poached raspberries. Of course it ain't cheap – expect to pay in excess of €100 for the eight-course tasting menu, plus another €60 with a selection of wines – but when all is said and done, it's cracking value. In fact, why not go the whole hog and stop the night in one of the house's supremely comfortable rooms? Then you can start all over again with a fabulous breakfast the next morning.

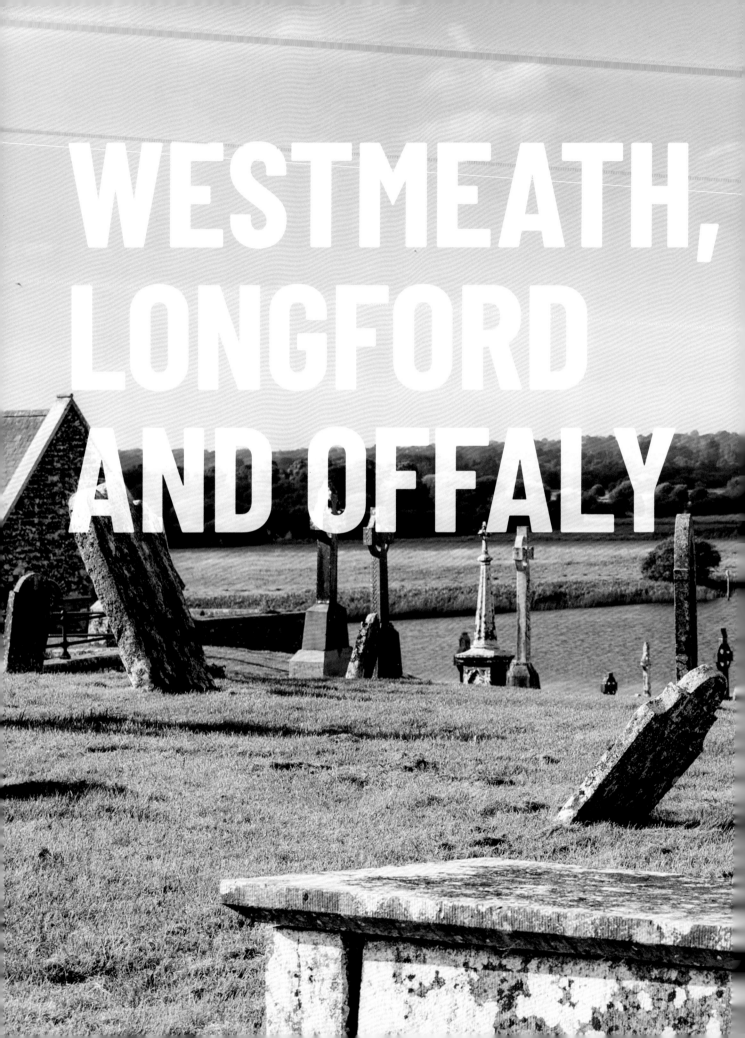

WESTMEATH, LONGFORD AND OFFALY

The Goddess Ériu

Medieval re-enactments

Dressing up in medieval costume

The Hill of Uisneach

HILL OF UISNEACH

Uisneach (roughly pronounced 'ish-knack') is the sacred and mythological centre of Ireland; site of Bealtaine fires and Druidical ceremonies. Situated in Rathnew, County Westmeath, at 596ft above sea level, there are views of the central plain of Ireland with twenty counties visible. Surviving monuments and relics range in date from Neolithic, early Bronze Age and the Medieval period, including a megalithic tomb, burial mounds, enclosures, standing stones, holy wells and a ceremonial road. Uisneach is the mythological resting place of Ériu, goddess of Ireland who gave her name to the country, and it was the original seat of the High Kings of Ireland before this passed to Tara in neighbouring County Meath. It remained the meeting point for the ancient provinces where deals were struck. It was linked to Tara by a ceremonial road, a section of which remains today. Today the site is still used to celebrate the coming of summer with the Bealtaine festival, when a fire is lit on the hill and there is music, art installations, talks and names. Guided tours of the site can be booked providing valuable interpretation of Uisneach's features and history.

The whiskey barrels

The nineteenth-century water wheel

The old distillery building

A glass of fine Kilbeggan whiskey

KILBEGGAN DISTILLERY

Kilbeggan Distillery is the oldest operational distillery in Ireland and, apart from an interlude in the twentieth century, has been turning out some of the nation's finest whiskey for over two hundred years. While lesser known, this County Westmeath distillery roundly predates the household names of Jameson and Bushmills and should be a must-see for whiskey lovers. It may not surprise you that the booze business contains its fair share of controversy and criminality, of which Kilbeggan claims a respectable slice – from wanted lawbreakers under alias looking to flip its whiskey on English black markets, to the execution of the original founder's son for his part in the failed revolt of 1798. Doggedly beating back financial woes from every angle over its illustrious lifespan, today you'll find Kilbeggan to be a welcoming and fully functioning distillery. Deep biscuity aromas will greet your arrival along with the rushing waters of the River Brosna, pouring through the distillery's nineteenth-century water wheel still used to power machinery inside. A 1hr 30min 'Distillery Experience' tour starts with a whiskey cocktail taster and ends with a four-glass masterclass in whiskey sampling, making for a warming educational experience. In-between drinks you'll enjoy stories re-telling the distillery's fascinating history alongside rich insights into their unique distillation process.

The distillery vats from the outside

Sean's place

Seans Bar

Irelands Oldest Pub
As Listed In
GUINNESS Book Of
World Records

SEAN'S BAR

Dating from 900AD, *Sean's Bar* is the oldest in Ireland and is located only a few steps from Athlone's Norman castle. Renovations during the 1970s revealed that the walls were constructed from wattle and wicker, a section of which can be seen in the bar behind a glass panel, the remainder being housed for preservation in Ireland's National Museum. With such a pedigree, the atmosphere does not disappoint, while the open fire and sawdust floor will mean you will gladly settle into this cosy bar for the evening. Outside at the rear of the bar a sheltered beer garden has been created which overlooks the River Shannon. Explore the neighbouring streets which are full of bars, restaurants and independent shops. Maybe work up a thirst by visiting Athlone Castle, where you can learn about the history of this important fortification on the River Shannon through interactive displays and demonstrations. Or take a walk along the banks of the Shannon and watch the boats come and go from the Marina.

SEAN'S BAR
IRISH WHISKEY

SEAN'S BAR
IRISH WHISKEY

Enjoy the terrace on a sunny day

The historic pub

Relics on display in Athlone Castle

The beer garden

CORLEA TRACKWAY

In the boglands of south County Longford, a *togher* or bog road was discovered in the 1980s in an area where peat was industrially harvested. This pathway, constructed from heavy planks of oak, was dated using dendrochronological (tree-ring dating) testing to 148BC–contemporaneous with the Siege of Carthage by the Romans. The Corlea Trackway is the largest bog road to have been discovered in Europe. At the visitor centre in Corlea, you can view an 18m-stretch of the trackway in a hall specially designed to preserve it, as well as murals and displays showing people and objects of the era, to give you a real sense of how people would have lived at that time. It is thought that the trackway may have been part of a ceremonial highway connecting the Hill of Uisneach (see page 60) with Rathcroghan (see page 177). The terrain would have been dangerous and impassable for much of the year, being mainly bog, quicksand and ponds. It has been suggested that people wanted to get into the bog for ceremonial reasons, rather than travel across it. The trackway remained in use for only a few years before sinking under its own weight and was thus preserved by the bog. During your visit you can take a walk across a preserved bog nearby.

Walking over the bog

The visitor centre

Original track

Exhibitions explain the history of the site

The motte

Dressed for knighthood

The heritage centre

A statue of St Patrick watches over the site

GRANARD MOTTE AND BAILEY

In the north-east of County Longford you will find the highest motte in Ireland at 534ft above sea level, built circa 1199 by Norman knight Richard de Tuite after he was granted lands by Henry II. De Tuite was later made Lord Chief Justice of Ireland. The fortification was erected on and within a pre-existing hillfort as part of an initiative to extend Norman control over Ireland. Originally a timber tower surrounded by a palisade and ditch, Granard Motte and Bailey would have enclosed animals and soldiers. Today of course the timber structures are gone, leaving behind a great flat-topped earthen mound. The summit gives views of five lakes and nine counties. Myths have persisted regarding the hollow within the mound, which some believe contains a castle or gold. Indeed, in 2017 a large hole was found dug into the side of the mound, presumably an effort to find the buried treasure! Nearby is the Knights and Conquests heritage centre which is a great family attraction. Here you can dress in Norman clothes, receive a Norman name and discover and dig for artefacts in the Norman display room. You will also meet a Norman knight who will explain the weapons of the period, and maybe even let you wield one.

The castle grounds have many walking trails

BIRR CASTLE

Astronomy, engineering, botany, history-all feature at Birr Castle in County Offaly. It is home to the Great Telescope, the largest telescope in the world when it was built in the 1840s, alongside fifty champion trees and reputedly the largest children's tree house in the country. A castle was originally built on the site during the Anglo-Norman period; following several instances of destruction and rebuilding, the current iteration of the building dates from the 1800s, although walls from the very first building still survive. The castle has been home to the Parsons family for centuries and is still occupied as a private family home, therefore tours of the house are restricted to the summer months and must be prebooked. The grounds alone are worth seeing however; there is an incredible variety of trees and plants, reflecting the plant hunting of the Parsons family. Mapped trails will take you through some of the fifty hectares of grounds with varied landscape including rivers, waterfalls, a lake as well as formal gardens. There are over 5000 plant species as well as the world's tallest box hedge. The ancient oak trees are a must-see. Plans are now underway to create the largest grove of giant redwoods outside California. The Science Centre holds a collection of early electrical and engineering equipment, as well as early astronomical and photographic instruments used by the family.

This quirky building houses the Science Centre

The Great Telescope

The castle

The Science Centre

The high crosses are hundreds of years old

Views over the graveyard to the Shannon

A boat across to Clonmacnoise

The remains of the monastery

A high cross

CLONMACNOISE

While Clonmacnoise is a well-known tourist attraction of the Midlands, travelling there by boat offers a truly impressive view of the ruined monastery from the River Shannon as you approach. Cruises can be booked from a number of towns along the Shannon such as Athlone and Carrick-on-Shannon. The monastery at Clonmacnoise was founded in the sixth century by St Ciaran, and drew scholars from all over Europe, becoming an important seat of learning. Unfortunately, it also became very attractive to the Vikings and Normans, whose attacks contributed to its decline, culminating in its final abandonment in the 1500s. The ruins include a cathedral, several churches, two round towers and three high crosses, and all have been sensitively conserved. An interesting feature of the cathedral is a doorway known as the Whispering Arch which it is said was used for confession by lepers – they could stand on one side and whisper their sins, and the structure of the doorway would allow the monk standing on the other side to hear without getting too close. Visitors today can try it for themselves. The Interpretative Centre on-site provides some history and has some archaeological artefacts on display.

LOUGH BOORA DISCOVERY PARK

Lough Boora Discovery Park is the result of the rehabilitation of the land following decades of peat harvesting for the supply of Ireland's power stations and homes. While the destruction of Ireland's raised peat bogs is certainly nothing to be proud of, the example provided by Lough Boora in Offaly of how the land can be restored with both nature and community in mind is inspiring. This free amenity not only provides walking and cycling trails through a variety of landscapes, but it is also a sanctuary for a variety of flora and fauna. The park boasts an archaeological site dating to the Mesolithic Age providing evidence that the Midlands of Ireland were colonised 3000 years earlier than previously believed. Maps can be collected from the small visitor centre and café showing the trails which vary in length, can be walked or cycled and include an excellent fairy trail in the woods for the smaller trekkers. Sculptures dotted around the park are inspired by the natural and industrial history of the surroundings, many of which are designed to weather and evolve over time. Lakes were created here following the end of peat extraction which have now been developed, naturalised and stocked with fish making these lakes very popular with anglers. Many water birds have now made the bog their home and over 130 bird species have been recorded in the area. Bird hides are located throughout the site.

Man-made lakes

Aerial view of the discovery park

Feeding the swans

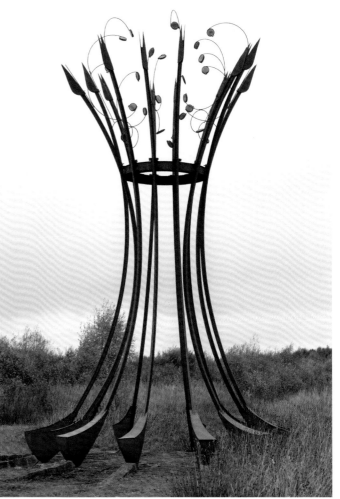
Sculptures are dotted around the park

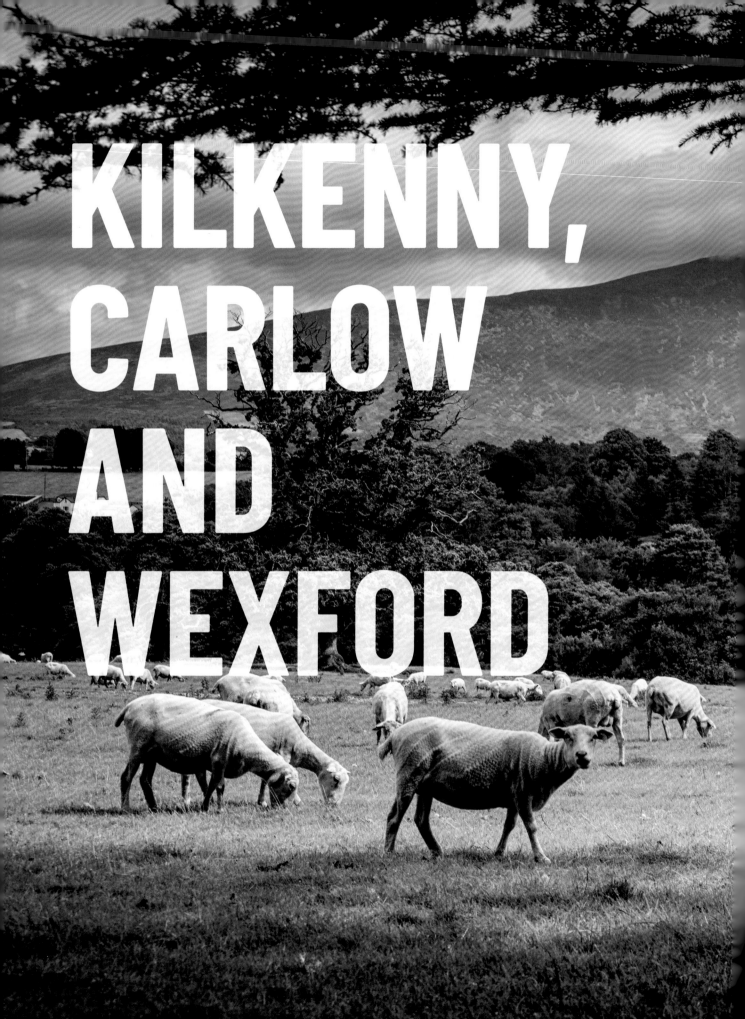

KILKENNY, CARLOW AND WEXFORD

The museum

MEDIEVAL MILE

See the historic sights of Kilkenny city on a walking tour and use the Medieval Mile Museum as your starting point. Formerly St Mary's Church, it is now a museum with 800 years of Kilkenny's history under its roof as well as being a beautiful vantage point to see the city (check out the panoramic window in the Kilkenny Room). From here, take a guided tour or wander out by yourself to see sights such as Kilkenny Castle and Rothe House and Gardens; the latter is well worth a visit during the summer, especially in August for the Kilkenny Arts Festival when there's a whole calendar of concerts alongside pop-up galleries with local art for sale. The tour is worth the ticket as you'll get local stories and history as well as interesting nuggets of local lore, such as tales of witchcraft in Kyteler's Inn. Afterwards, pop into *The Hole in the Wall*, the city's oldest and quirkiest bar for a tipple. If still in town and hungry to see more, there is also the Smithwick's Brewery, St Canice's Cathedral and Round Tower (the winding steps to the top are not for the claustrophobic), and across the river, the modern Butler Art Gallery.

Kilkenny Castle

St Canice's Cathedral

The Medieval Mile Museum

Ancient statues on display in the museum

INISTIOGE

Just a 25km drive from Kilkenny City lies the delightful and historic village of Inistioge (pronounced 'innish-teague'). Situated on the River Nore with an attractive eighteenth-century stone bridge with ten arches, the historic village is home to pleasant pubs, an antique shop, art gallery and a café. Unsurprisingly, it has been used on more than one occasion as a set for major film productions due to the many fine period houses built in the eighteenth and nineteenth centuries that line the village square. One unusual sight is the location of two churches, St Mary's Church of Ireland dating from medieval times and the Roman Catholic church of St Colmcille standing side by side. Behind the churches are the ruins of a thirteenth-century Augustan Priory and on the hillside is a mausoleum where Mary Tighe of Woodstock House is buried. Woodstock House itself is up the steep hill leading from the village, through imposing gates at the end of a long driveway. There's a fee to enter the carpark that covers entry to the gardens. Now sadly just a shell, it has beautiful landscaped gardens and a lovely woodland playground for kids, as well as a Victorian teahouse (open in peak season) to enjoy. For a scenic walk, leave your car in the village and walk up, taking the road to the left of the entry and stroll down to the waterfall from where you can do a long loop back to the village along tree-lined river paths.

The river Nore runs through Inistioge

The village square has many Georgian houses

/iews of the village

Woodstock's Monkey Puzzle Walk

The aroma from the rhododendron is intoxicating

Altamont is famed for its roses

The gardens are full of wonderful specimen plants

A resident peacock

ALTAMONT GARDENS

Altamont is often referred to as the jewel in Ireland's gardening crown. Situated just outside Tullow, County Carlow, it boasts forty acres of old-world manicured lawns, specimen trees, and informal gardens inspired by the style of Irish horticulturalist William Robinson. Exploring these gardens is easily done on foot, with various walking trails mapping out a route around the lake, Bog Garden, and Ice Age Glen, a riverside woodland walk under impressive oaks. Another trail, the Temple Walk, leads up to a small temple overlooking fields and farmland as far as the eye can see; a place to pause for a moment and watch the barley sway in the breeze. Visit in July and you'll be treated to a beautiful herbaceous border in full bloom. Over 60m-long, it is packed with dahlias, achillea and roses, to name but a few. On site you'll also find a nursery and Sugar & Spice café with indoor and outdoor seating; the latter is dotted with pergolas and large umbrellas to keep the summer sun (or rain) from the tables.

VISUAL

One of the country's leading contemporary arts spaces, VISUAL in County Carlow offers an exciting platform for the arts in the southeast. Established in 2009, this Centre for Contemporary Art and the 350-seat George Bernard Shaw Theatre offers a brilliant year-round programme of events, talks and changing exhibitions, as well as artist residencies. There is a cinema featuring the best artistically acclaimed films, theatre productions of great plays, as well as musicals, regular comedy shows and music concerts by mainly Irish solo artists and bands. The on-site bar and restaurant is inviting for pre-theatre drinks and dining. The striking modernist building itself is formed of a series of cubes on a concrete base, clad in opaque glass, and is situated in the centre of the town on the grounds of St Patrick's College. The building and installations are completely accessible in line with the space's ethos of art being available to all.

The modernist exterior

Ancient trees line the Yew Walk

HUNTINGTON CASTLE

There are many delightful things about Huntington Castle in County Carlow, not least the friendly, roaming peacock. Built in the 1600s, the castle is privately owned by the Durdin Robertsons, who live there and open it to the public. Take a guided castle tour to explore the original Tapestry Room and all its fineries, the conservatory with its magnificent grape vine on the ceiling (a gift to Anne Boleyn that came from Hampton Court Palace in London) and take delight in stories of the Temple of the Goddess deep in the castle's dungeon. In the grounds, follow the paths in the formal Italian Parterre, breathe in the scent on the sumptuous rose walk (when in bloom), enjoy the calm Water Gardens and appreciate the changing seasons in the gardens all year round. Youngsters will enjoy the cute Woodland Playground, complete with an obstacle course, play huts, and diggers - bound to be the inspiration of many adventures. The tearooms serve locally baked sweet treats and refreshments in the seventeenth-century barn next to the castle, beside which is a gift shop. During the summer and clement weather you can sit out in the pleasant courtyard (picnics are not permitted on the grounds). Just beware that peacock, he has quite a weakness for scones.

Perfectly manicured lawns surround the castle

The castle up close

The castle is located in the midst of stunnning countryside

The Water Gardens

Watersports are a natural choice here

Walking the dunes

Miles of sandy beach, perfect for leisurely walks

Raven Point Wood

CURRACLOE BEACH

Curracloe strand, 11km northeast of Wexford Harbour, is a totally unspoiled, pristine stretch of beach that runs for 10km along some of the country's loveliest coastline. Wedged between untamed dunes and the Atlantic Ocean, it 'stood in' for the Normandy beaches, namely Omaha Beach, as the site of the D-Day landings when Steven Spielberg filmed *Saving Private Ryan* here in 1998. Extending south is the Raven Nature Reserve, an expanse of dunes and a 600-acre pine forest that stretches down to Raven Point at the mouth of the estuary. The easy 6.5km looped walk through the forest trail is lovely and offers a chance to spot some of the conservation area's protected wildlife such as the red squirrel. Bird enthusiasts will delight - species including the Greenland White-fronted goose, cormorant, red-throated diver, grey plover, common scoter and sanderling can all be spotted here. In spring, keep an ear out for the noisy natterjack toad, in summer, delight in the prettiest butterflies. Take to the waves or the sand, breathe in the salt-tanged air and enjoy one of Ireland's finest beaches.

Carrigfoyle Lake

FORTH MOUNTAIN

Just a couple of miles from Wexford town, Forth Mountain's towering outcrop rises almost 800ft above the land and packs more than just views into an accessible, beautiful hike. Visitors to this overlooked peak will be treated to expansive views of the county, along with the ruins of eighteenth-century cottages and a natural grotto to explore. Lake Carrigfoyle sits at the base of the 'mountain' with clear blue waters and sandy shores, looking more like North America or Italy than south-eastern Ireland. Named after the ancient Celtic tribe who once claimed this land, there's history in this earth – from some of the oldest geology to be found in Ireland, over 500 million years in age, to a pivotal battle in the 1798 Rebellion. Also emerqinq from the qround is new evidence of the 'lost town of Carrig', site of one of the first Norman fortresses in Ireland and a town of over one hundred houses buried and forgotten. Site of the famous Battle of Three Rocks – a major victory for the ultimately unsuccessful United Irishmen of the late eighteenth-century – the rocky slopes of Forth Mountain facilitated a bloody ambush against the British with musket and pike. It's easy to trace the footsteps of those Wexford fighting men along the Three Rocks Trail, taking in the remains of both battle and burial grounds while surrounded by breathtaking views and a wealth of natural delights.

The servants tunnel

JOHNSTOWN CASTLE

A 900-hundred-year-old Gothic Revival castle standing proudly on 120 acres, Johnstown Castle is a wonderful piece of Irish history in County Wexford that is worth exploring. Withstanding the test of time in superb order, the castle was fist given to the Esmonde family as a thank you for the role they played in the Norman Invasion of Ireland in 1169. While its towers date back to the 1170s, its neo-Gothic looks came about in the nineteenth century when it was remodelled by the Grogan family. Guided tours of its interior offer a taste of life in bygone times, from the rare servants' tunnel and kitchens to the lavish upstairs quarters. Outside, the ornamental gardens invite serene walks among sculptured topiary and flowers, and summer picnics in the sunken garden. Meander along lakeside paths and through woodland teeming with wildlife. A four-acre walled garden and its hothouses that were first formed in 1844 are being restored to their former splendour. The Irish Agricultural Museum on site explores farming and rural life in wonderful detail. Pop into the café in the visitor centre for refreshments and souvenirs and grab some food to feed the resident peacocks. Year-round, there is a host of regular events ranging from jazz concerts to evening bat walks, tours and talks on its resident bees, vintage car rallies and everything in between.

The first floor

Pretty garden trails

The castle

The male boudoir

WATERFORD AND TIPPERARY

COUMSHINGAUN LOUGH

Here lies a little realm quite literally hidden in the folds of the land. Tucked within steep craggy cliffs on three sides, this paradise is kept off the well-beaten path due to the challenging hike needed to complete it. Just over half an hour's drive from Waterford City, Coumshingaun Lough is easy to find, but difficult to master. The route is three to four hours in total but involves clambering and scrambling over some rough terrain — not to mention coming close to sheer cliffs at times. Climbing up to the plateau and entering the vast gateway of this horseshoe, on a clear day the typically placid waters of the lough will be a mirror filled with mighty cliffs and crags. Up on the ridges await spectacular views of the lake and surrounding country, stretching into infinity on three sides and to the sea on another. A few words of caution, however; good walking equipment, fitness and the ability to navigate are strongly recommended, especially if visibility is affected by the weather. Completing the circular route clockwise is also a sensible choice. Mahon Falls offers an equally delightful but more accessible alternative just a few minutes away. It's a perfect family hike, with a moderate difficulty and the majestic waterfalls as a constant waypoint.

The clear waters of the lake

The Comeragh Mountains

Views over Coumshingaun Lough

Mahon Falls

Inside Ballyvoyle Tunnel

Approaching Dungarvan

Kilmacthomas Viaduct

Ballyvoyle Tunnel

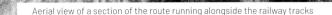

WATERFORD GREENWAY

A car-free cycle path created along a disused railway line, the Waterford Greenway is one of the country's best car-free cycling and walking paths, encompasing lovely countryside every bit of the way. The 46km-long greenway offers hours of recreational cycling or walking, along Ireland's southeast from Waterford city, through Kilmacthomas and onto the stunning coastal town of Dungarvan. Divided into six sections of varying lengths and difficulty, whichever section you choose, it's a wonderful day out for all fitness levels and ages. Recommended routes for children include the short Killoteran to Kilmeaden section which allows you to hop off and jump on the Suir Valley Heritage train, get great views of the River Suir and drop into lovely Mount Congreve Gardens or the longer Durrow to Clonee section which takes you through the Ballyvoyle Tunnel, a 400m-long tunnel. The longer sections are more challenging but each section has something to offer, be it a stop at a pub along the way, a Norman castle or a bridge or viaduct with stunning views. For the fittest among you, the whole thing can be cycled in one go, staying overnight on arrival or arranging a pick up at the other end.

The amusement park

Tramore is a surfer's haven

The Doneraile Walk

Seaside fish and chips

TRAMORE

Tramore, once a one-stop shop for cheap n' cheerful fish and chips on its sandy beach with the giddy soundtrack of fairground music and shrieks from the roller coaster in the background, is today undergoing somewhat of a transformation. The lure of its amusement park with its candy floss and bumper cars, has now the added appeal as a surfer's hangout and mini foodie haven. Sign up to lessons at one of the surf schools along the beach or follow the lunchtime crowds to award-winning café *Mezze* for vegetarian Middle Eastern fare, *Molly's Café* for the best coffee in town or the much-applauded seafood lunch haunt *Beach House* (by the same owners as Fish Shop in Dublin). For simple fish and chips, *Dooly's* is great. Afterwards, a jump from the diving board in Newtown Cove may not be for the faint of heart but it's certain to blast away the cobwebs. Those with less of a daredevil streak can wander along to The Guillamene, Newtown's twin cove and an equally popular swimming hole.

The beach

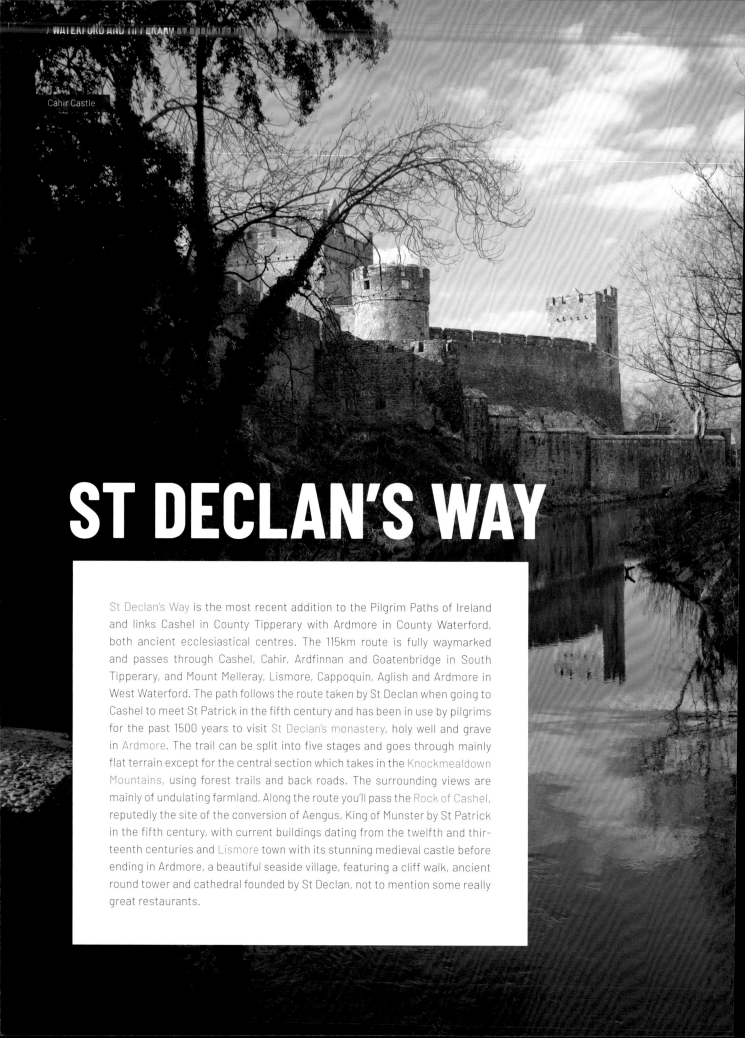

Cahir Castle

ST DECLAN'S WAY

St Declan's Way is the most recent addition to the Pilgrim Paths of Ireland and links Cashel in County Tipperary with Ardmore in County Waterford, both ancient ecclesiastical centres. The 115km route is fully waymarked and passes through Cashel, Cahir, Ardfinnan and Goatenbridge in South Tipperary, and Mount Melleray, Lismore, Cappoquin, Aglish and Ardmore in West Waterford. The path follows the route taken by St Declan when going to Cashel to meet St Patrick in the fifth century and has been in use by pilgrims for the past 1500 years to visit St Declan's monastery, holy well and grave in Ardmore. The trail can be split into five stages and goes through mainly flat terrain except for the central section which takes in the Knockmealdown Mountains, using forest trails and back roads. The surrounding views are mainly of undulating farmland. Along the route you'll pass the Rock of Cashel, reputedly the site of the conversion of Aengus, King of Munster by St Patrick in the fifth century, with current buildings dating from the twelfth and thirteenth centuries and Lismore town with its stunning medieval castle before ending in Ardmore, a beautiful seaside village, featuring a cliff walk, ancient round tower and cathedral founded by St Declan, not to mention some really great restaurants.

Hore Abbey, Cashel

The Cliff Walk, Ardmore

Ardfinnan, County Tipperary

The Round Tower, Ardmore

ATHASSEL ABBEY

The largest medieval priory in the country, twelfth century Athassel Abbey is well off the beaten path and offers the chance to wander alone through 800 years of beautiful history on the banks of River Suir. It was founded by an order of Augustine monks, with the support of William de Burgh, and was dedicated to St Edmund until its dissolution in 1537. Historical and archaeological evidence tells us that the abbey formed the heart of its own urban community at its peak, with perhaps 2000 people coming to live in the surrounding town. A cultural and economic magnet, so too did it attract attention during times of conflict – resulting in it being twice burned and the town destroyed by the sixteenth century. Set in a verdant four acre site, the priory has been battered and smoothed under the tides of centuries. Though a crumbling stone shell without roof, glass or, in many cases, intact walls, its majesty shines through time. It's clear this place once had the care and love of many monks, attendants, citizens and other clergy who once roamed its hallways, cloisters and gardens. Found in the middle of quiet pastures and usually accessed by hopping a low wall or squeezing through an old gate, Athassel feels like a well-kept secret. You'll likely have nobody but yourself for company in this utterly serene place.

The abbey remains

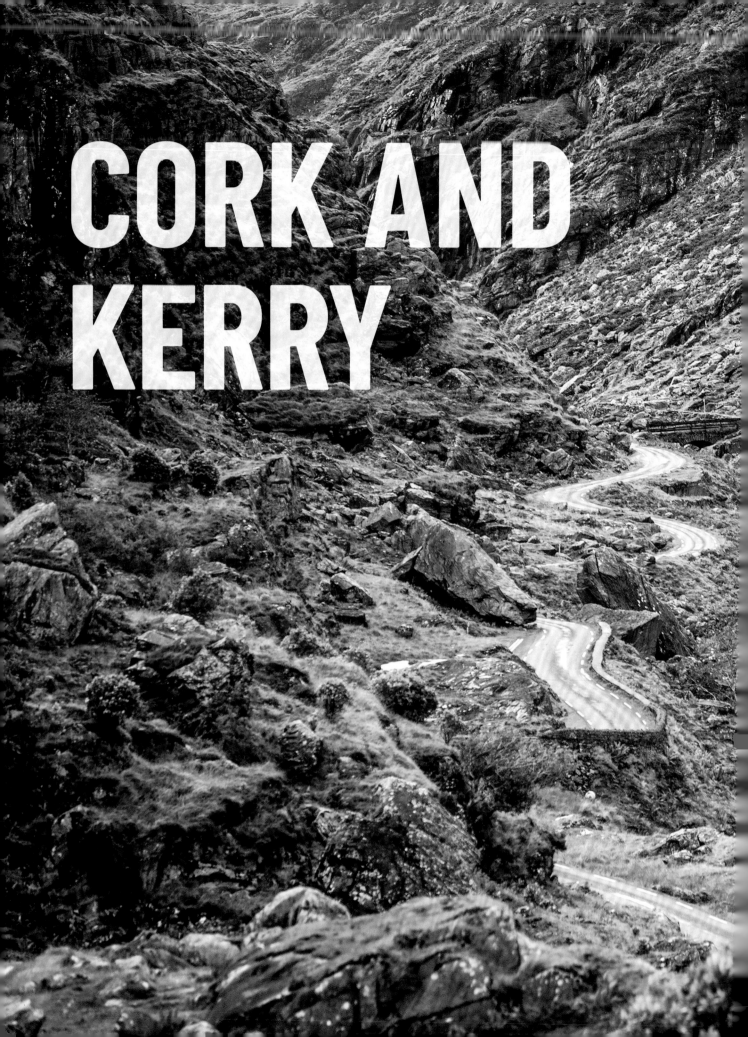

CORK AND KERRY

The freshest of local catches for sale

Irish smoked salmon

Fine craft butchers

Cashel blue cheese

THE ENGLISH MARKET

Food fabulous food, the eighteenth-century English Market slap bang in the middle of Cork city is bursting with mouth-watering stalls that give credence to the city's claim to be the food capital of Ireland. Established in 1788, the attractive red-brick heritage building in which it is housed is a joy to visit in itself with its lofty arched ceiling and airy space. Indeed, this is one of Europe's best covered markets and, oh, is it a sensuous joy to explore. Brimming with artisinal produce, much of which is sourced locally, its fresh and eclectic stalls are a delight. There's seafood caught locally in Ballycotton, cured meats, local cheeses, olives, bread, handmade chocolate, fine pastries, butcher's shops, vegetable stalls, spices and condiments, fine wines, oils, and more. Fill your larder or source a picnic to take to the park or to the sea. Or eat on site, lured in by the tantalising aromas that waft from the delis and stalls. Open Monday to Saturday from 8am to 6pm.

The market

SPIKE ISLAND

Spike Island in Cork Harbour can be reached by taking a ferry from the town of Cobh, a half-hour drive outside of Cork city. Last year a new immersive 'augmented reality app' was introduced on the island with fifteen stopping points enabling visitors to re-live important historical events and see characters come alive. The island certainly has a colourful history. Beginning with the St Mochuda Monastery (600 AD), followed by the construction of a military fortress, later to become the world's largest prison capable of holding over 2000 inmates in the 1850s. Over a long period of time this prison was used on four separate occasions, in the 1600s, 1800s, during the War of Independence and, most recently, in 1985 as a place to hold young offenders. By taking a guided tour with a specially trained storyteller you can explore more than twelve museums and exhibitions, prison cells, discreet tunnels, passages and an 1850s punishment block. After this intensive taste of incarceration, it's probably time to get a large dose of fresh air and take yourself off on the Ring of Spike scenic walking trail.

GOUGANE BARRA

It is no exaggeration to say that your first view of St Finbarr's Oratory on the lake at Gougane Barra will take your breath away. Nestled in a valley of the Shehy Mountains, this special place is a haven of peace and tranquillity, where the combination of mountain, lake and forest will calm and refresh the soul. A place of worship was first founded on this site by St Finbarr, patron saint of Cork, in the sixth century on an island in the lake, close to the source of the River Lee. The island is now connected to the shore by a causeway allowing access to the eighteenth century Oratory which was built near to the site of the original buildings. Nearby are the ruins of a seventeenth-century hermitage which feature stations of the cross. The surrounding hills are home to a 340-acre forest park which has recently seen extensive replanting with native tree species. Choose from six walking trails depending on your fitness level and discover beautiful vistas of the valley as well as waterfalls and gentle river walks. Treat yourself to a stay at the Gougane Barra Hotel, a family-run bolthole which really is a home from home and is right on the lakeshore. Wake up early to catch the mist rising over the water, a magical sight.

GLENGARRIFF

Almost as far west in Cork as you can get, just on the border with Kerry, the drive to Glengarriff is almost as enchanting as the end destination. Follow slow, winding roads bordered by mountains and a sea fed by the Gulf Stream, allowing for regular stops for passing sheep, as you journey to this pretty village with its exotic flora and fauna and sparkling blue sea. There is a lot to enjoy here: the Sessile oak Nature Reserve and Pooleen swimming spot, the harbour for sailing and kayaking, gorgeous Garinish Island with its house and Harold Peto Italianate gardens, the Bamboo Park, and Ewe Gallery and Sculpture Garden... Or take to the waters for deep-sea fishing or a marine wildlife tour - and count oyster catchers, egrets, sea eagles, cormorants and grey heron in abundance. On and offshore, the huge colony of harbour seals that calls Glengarriff home is a joy to observe. When the day is done, lunch, dinner or at the very least a drink in the longstanding institution that is *The Blue Loo* on the Main Street is most definitely a must.

Drinks outside *The Blue Loo*

The gardens on Garinish Island

Seals lazing offshore

Enjoying sunny days at *Harrington's* village pub

The castle at night

ROSS CASTLE

Nestled in the heart of Kerry and just minutes from the delightful town of Killarney, Ross Castle is a classic example of the Irish fortified tower house built in the fifteenth century. The ancestral seat of Irish clan O'Donoghue perches on the shores of glittering Lough Leane – the Lake of Learning – and offers a unique insight into the tumultuous fifteenth to seventeenth century period of the country's history. Explorable only through an excellent, in-depth guided tour and offering magnificent views across the Killarney National Park, Ross Castle is home to legend, prophecy and tales of Cromwellian resistance. Walk beneath the shadows of defensive parapets and under arrow slits before ascending a fortified spiral staircase studded with vicious murder holes, entering the lives of the Irish chieftains who feasted, governed and fell from power within these thick stone walls. Happen by on the first morning of May (every seventh year) and you might even witness the rise of the ethereal O'Donoghue Mór from the deep waters of the lake, astride a mighty white stallion. Ross Castle is well combined with a trip to nearby Innisfallen Abbey. Cloister yourself among the trees and ruins of this serene monastic site, after being dropped off on a small island in the centre of the myth-steeped lake, to enjoy a perfectly secluded couple of hours.

The castle walls

Romantic rowboats ready to take out

The Killarney National Park walking trail

An original doorway at Ross Castle

The Kerry Way walking trail

Torc Waterfall, Killarney

Old Weir Bridge, Killarney Lakes

Routes are well signposted

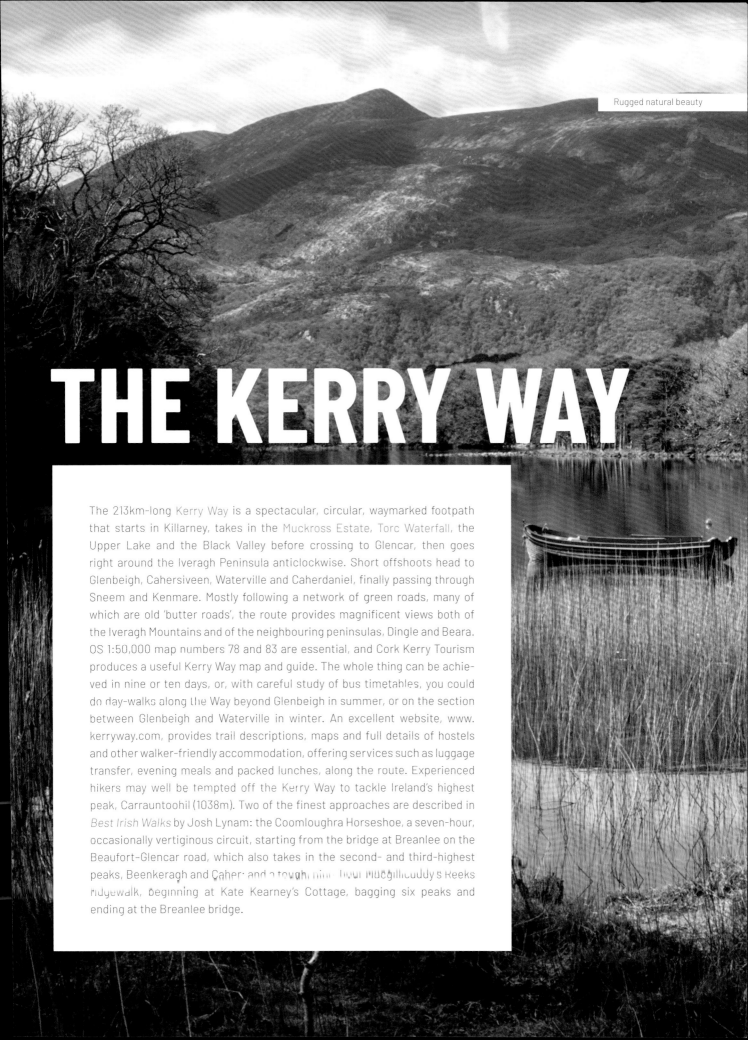

THE KERRY WAY

The 213km-long Kerry Way is a spectacular, circular, waymarked footpath that starts in Killarney, takes in the Muckross Estate, Torc Waterfall, the Upper Lake and the Black Valley before crossing to Glencar, then goes right around the Iveragh Peninsula anticlockwise. Short offshoots head to Glenbeigh, Cahersiveen, Waterville and Caherdaniel, finally passing through Sneem and Kenmare. Mostly following a network of green roads, many of which are old 'butter roads', the route provides magnificent views both of the Iveragh Mountains and of the neighbouring peninsulas, Dingle and Beara. OS 1:50,000 map numbers 78 and 83 are essential, and Cork Kerry Tourism produces a useful Kerry Way map and guide. The whole thing can be achieved in nine or ten days, or, with careful study of bus timetables, you could do day-walks along the Way beyond Glenbeigh in summer, or on the section between Glenbeigh and Waterville in winter. An excellent website, www.kerryway.com, provides trail descriptions, maps and full details of hostels and other walker-friendly accommodation, offering services such as luggage transfer, evening meals and packed lunches, along the route. Experienced hikers may well be tempted off the Kerry Way to tackle Ireland's highest peak, Carrauntoohil (1038m). Two of the finest approaches are described in *Best Irish Walks* by Josh Lynam: the Coomloughra Horseshoe, a seven-hour, occasionally vertiginous circuit, starting from the bridge at Breanlee on the Beaufort-Glencar road, which also takes in the second- and third-highest peaks, Beenkeragh and Caher; and a tough, nine-hour MacGillicuddy's Reeks ridgewalk, beginning at Kate Kearney's Cottage, bagging six peaks and ending at the Breanlee bridge.

Island life

Aerial view of the island

An original cottage

Dinghies ferry passengers to boats offshore from the jetty

Quiet roads offer stunning views

THE BLASKET ISLANDS

Just off Slea Head lie the Blaskets, dramatic island mountains with steep, gashed sides. Despite its inhospitable appearance, the largest island, Great Blasket (*An Blascaod Mór*), was inhabited by up to two hundred people for at least three centuries until 1953, when, with no school, shop, priest or doctor, it was finally abandoned. Because of their isolation, however, the islanders maintained a rich oral tradition in the Irish language, which in the early twentieth century, encouraged by visiting scholars, evolved into a remarkable body of written literature. Works such as *An tOileánach* (*The Islandman*) by Tomás Ó Criomhthain, *Fiche Blian ag Fás* (*Twenty Years A-Growing*) by Muiris Ó Súilleabháin and *Peig* by Peig Sayers (an oral account in Irish transcribed by her son) give a vivid insight into the hardships of life there. In the summer, boats to Great Blasket leave the pier on the south side of Dunquin in good weather every hour or so. There are multiple other tours that leave from Ventry (booking essential). Enjoy a guided cruise around the Blasket Islands in the afternoon, taking in the spectacular Cathedral Rocks on Inishnabro, puffins (in spring and early summer, depending on the weather), grey seals and red deer on Inishvickillane (and if you're lucky, basking sharks, whales and dolphins) or try a seven-hour guided cruise combined with a landing on Great Blasket. In addition, from Dingle town, tours run ferries to Great Blasket once a day.

LIMERICK
AND CLARE

FLYING BOAT & MARITIME MUSEUM

Foynes, a town on the southern bank of the Shannon Estuary in County Limerick, was an important port for over 160 years. Today it's still busy handling bulk container ships. However, its main claim to fame was the period between 1939 and 1945 when it became a base for air travel between the USA and Ireland, the only European Terminal at that time for transatlantic flights. The really interesting Flying Boat & Maritime Museum gives a great insight into all aspects of both the aviation and port story of Foynes. Officially opened by Irish film icon Maureen O'Hara in 1989 it has a dedicated exhibition space highlighting many aspects of her career. Visitors can then board the only replica in the world of a full-size Boeing 314 Clipper Flying Boat, view a major collection of aviation memorabilia, enter a weather room with original radio equipment and visit the reinstated control tower with views of the town and Shannon Estuary. The list of celebrities and VIPs who passed through the airport is quite impressive. Names such as Ernest Hemingway, Bob Hope and Humphrey Bogart plus numerous kings, queens and prime ministers from around the world are all documented or photographed during the period. In 1943 it was noticed passengers arriving were either cold or tired and a decision was made to serve them a hot coffee with a drop of whiskey and some cream. Irish Coffee, now famous around the world, was served for the very first time. In the Maritime Museum you will learn all about the history of Foynes Port and River Shannon, Ireland's longest river.

The tail of an early Boeing 747

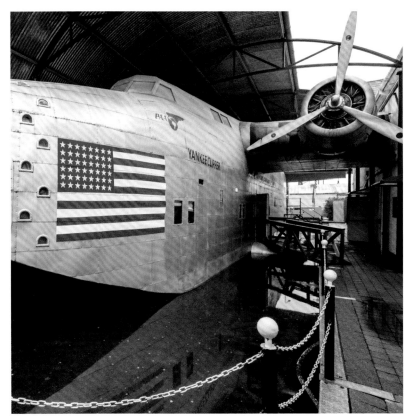

An aircraft on display

Working the control panels

Means of communication from the heyday

Outside the museum

LOUGH GUR

Ireland is overflowing with outstanding archaeological treasures due to its peaty and often waterlogged landscape, making ideal conditions for preserving ancient artefacts and settlements over thousands of years. With so many sites to explore during your time in Ireland, if you had to pick the best? Lough Gur will be near the top of most lists. Scattered along shores, hills and woodlands ringing a magnificent lake, this collection of sites nestled in 'Limerick's Lake District' is an internationally significant archaeological zone. It's home to 136 monuments including Ireland's oldest stone circle, megalithic stone tombs, Bronze and Iron Age *crannógs*, early Christian hill forts, medieval castles and more. Start at the visitor centre to choose from professional guided tours or self-guided trail maps, as well as immersive multimedia exhibitions showcasing 6000 years of Irish history at Lough Gur. From hunter-gathers to the modern human, every step of the Irish people is recorded in this earth. There's something for everyone here, even if standing stones and crumbling fortresses don't get you up in the morning. A fairy trail will have kids diving into the mysteries of this place, while kayaking on the lake is a great way to soak in the ambience.

Starry nights over the lake

Entrance to the visitor centre

Relics found at the site

Aerial view of the stone circle

The leather-hulled boat

A lookout tower at the entry to the settlement

A conical hut

Re-enactments

A dolmen tomb

CRAGGAUNOWEN

Though the first thing you'll see when you arrive is a resplendent sixteenth century castle turned manor house, the open-air museum that is Craggaunowen in the east of County Clare has its focus further back into Ireland's past – much further. Just beyond the castle, through the veil of trees and a thousand years of history, emerges a prehistoric Celtic settlement, the crannóg. Surrounded by fifty acres of lush woodland and perched on an ancient man-made island, this award-winning recreation of a Bronze Age Irish ring fort faithfully replicates the exact living conditions and structures of the nation's early inhabitants. There's not a piece of cut masonry, electrical cable or plastic coating in sight at Craggaunowen. Dubbed 'the living history experience', visitors will cross into the heart of a lily covered lake and pass through the fort's single portal into an ancient realm; join costumed re-enactors spinning wool or making candles among the wide, conical huts and learn about how it was possible to live, fight and thrive in ancient Ireland. Subterranean passageways, Bronze Age industry, stone *dolmen* tombs and a leather-hulled boat – daringly used to prove the possibility of St Brendan's transatlantic travels in the sixth century – are just some of the treasures to be found in this unique place.

Brightly painted houses are typical in Clare

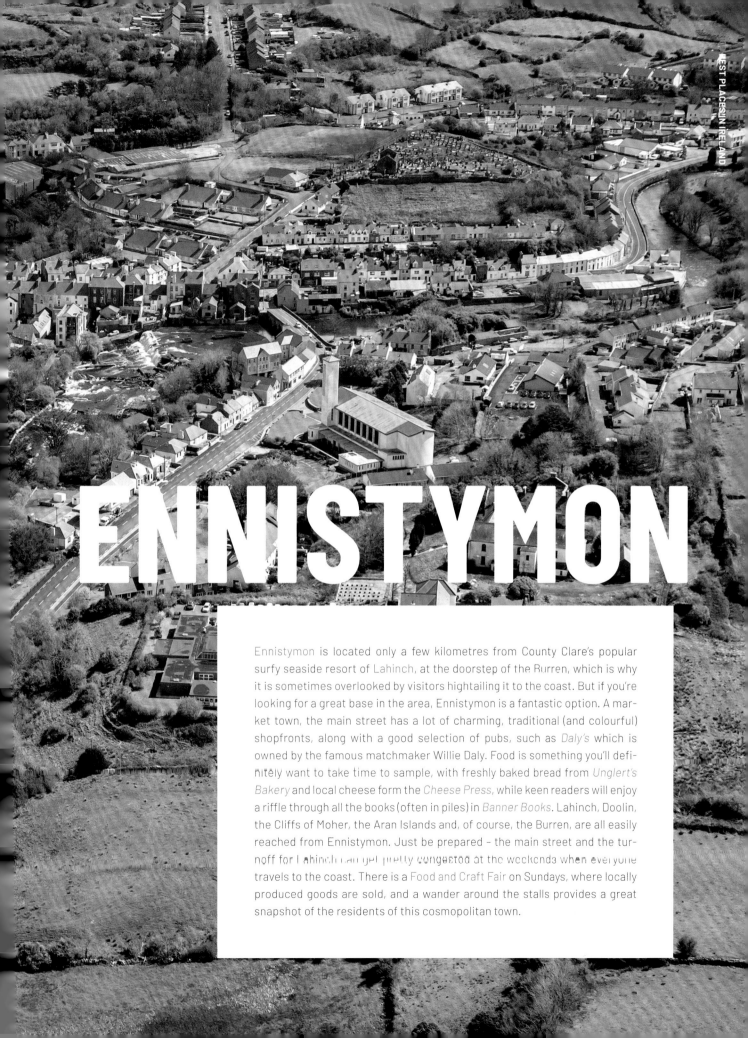

ENNISTYMON

Ennistymon is located only a few kilometres from County Clare's popular surfy seaside resort of Lahinch, at the doorstep of the Burren, which is why it is sometimes overlooked by visitors hightailing it to the coast. But if you're looking for a great base in the area, Ennistymon is a fantastic option. A market town, the main street has a lot of charming, traditional (and colourful) shopfronts, along with a good selection of pubs, such as *Daly's* which is owned by the famous matchmaker Willie Daly. Food is something you'll definitely want to take time to sample, with freshly baked bread from *Unglert's Bakery* and local cheese form the *Cheese Press*, while keen readers will enjoy a riffle through all the books (often in piles) in *Banner Books*. Lahinch, Doolin, the Cliffs of Moher, the Aran Islands and, of course, the Burren, are all easily reached from Ennistymon. Just be prepared – the main street and the turnoff for Lahinch can get pretty congested at the weekends when everyone travels to the coast. There is a Food and Craft Fair on Sundays, where locally produced goods are sold, and a wander around the stalls provides a great snapshot of the residents of this cosmopolitan town.

Monastic relics

The round tower

The visitor centre

The island graveyard

SCATTERY ISLAND

This tiny island is situated at the mouth of the Shannon Estuary, just off the West Clare coastal town of Kilrush. Founded in the sixth century by St Senan, Scattery Island became an important ecclesiastical site for hundreds of years. In 2017 a local family began operating daily boat trips from Kilrush Marina to the island, which quickly gained popularity. It's a short crossing and on arrival during the summer months visitors can enjoy a free tour of the main sites, including the remains of the monastic settlement, the cathedral and the five churches, as well as the deserted village, large round tower and a holy well. A building established in the 1930s as a post office still has the original post box.

There are two walking trails on the island, one of which brings you to the working lighthouse and a Napoleonic artillery battery. A small visitor centre in a restored cottage tells the history of island life through the years until 1978 when the last inhabitant left. When back on the mainland, in the proximity of Kilrush town is a Dolphin and Wildlife Centre, Museum of Irish Rural Life and the superb Vandeleur Walled Garden, an impeccably maintained botanic garden with pleasant woodland walks and bistro.

View of the mainland through the church window

Baked goods in the café

The entry to the chocolatier

Signposts lead the way

Marshmallows coated in chocolate

CHOCOLATE
ORBS
WITH
CRUNCHY MALT
CENTRES

HAZEL MOUNTAIN
CHOCOLATE

Calling all cacao connoisseurs. The award-winning Hazel Mountain Chocolate is situated in Oughtmama near Bellharbour on County Clare's Wild Atlantic Way route and is Ireland's only bean-to-bar chocolate factory. It uses sustainable and ethically sourced ingredients with a touch of imaginative panache – think milk chocolate with roasted hazelnuts and elderberry, 70% dark chocolate with seaweed, and chocolate-coated marshmallows. Enjoy more sweet treats in their architecturally designed café — voted one of Ireland's top ten — or al fresco if the sun is up. Browse some handmade Irish craft, handsome throws, homewares, and art in the Mercantile Store on site. The team offer guided tours and workshops as well. If you haven't eaten your fill, head to Monks in Ballyvaughan just a 10-minute drive away - it does a great seafood lunch or dinner - but book in advance, it's popular.

The stark mountain plateau

MULLAGHMORE MOUNTAIN

The Burren (*Bhoireann* in Irish) is one of the most unique areas in Ireland. It has the appearance of a 'Lunar landscape' but don't be deceived, there is an abundance of exotic plants to be discovered in the stark limestone rock, especially in spring and early summer. The Burren contains many castles, ancient churches, large stately homes and ancient wedge tombs spread throughout the region. No visit, however, to the wonderful Burren is complete without a trip to Mullaghmore Mountain. Travel down a minor country road from the village of Kilnaboy and a hulking rocky tabletop suddenly comes into view. It is quite breathtaking. After a short distance take a right down a small track to gain closer views of the front. Standing to admire the dramatic layered shape with the small Lough Gealain at its base, you immediately become aware why Mullaghmore is called a sacred mountain. It's an unmissable experience in what must be one of the few-remaining unspoilt landscapes in the country. The Burren National Park is here and a looped trail can be taken right to the top of Mullaghmore, for views of the dramatic limestone surroundings. Marvel at the profusion of orchids (many are rare) and the blue gentians, bloody cranesbill, and much more. If you have fond memories of the TV series *Father Ted* you're in luck because the 'Parochial House' used for filming is a short distance away. Although Glanquin Farmhouse (as it's formally called) is privately owned, photos may be taken of the outside from the front gate. Another attraction close by is the Burren Perfumery, a serene, sensory delight in the midst of a rugged landscape, with a tearoom and lovely outdoor seating.

The famed Parochial House

The vast lunar landscape

Views of Mullaghmore

Natural flora

LINNANE'S LOBSTER BAR

Northern Clare is famous for its Flaggy Shore (inspiration for Seamus Heaney's poem *Postscript*) and the rocky, rugged and almost otherworldly landscape that extends out from the Burren. If you are around New Quay, *Linnane's Lobster Bar* is a must. Located on the pier jutting into the sea, this secluded restaurant and bar has a menu bursting with the best of the local fishermen's catch of the day, and a wide selection of Irish craft beers to wash it all down with. Simply put, this is seafood heaven. The freshest of fresh lobster, muscles and oysters — all caught in the surrounding waters — are a wonderful testament to the region's sustainable fishing and natural abundance. Dine indoors by the fire during cold winters and watch boats come and go from the pier or sit outdoors in summer, basking in sunlight and fresh, tangy sea air. Linnane's is a member of the Burren Food Trail, so by visiting you also are supporting small, independent businesses that source regional products. Stretch your legs after your meal and take a stroll along the shoreline; one of nine sites of geological importance that bestow upon the Burren its UNESCO Global Geopark rating. Reservations are advisable to avoid disappointment.

Perfectly situated for fresh hauls

GALWAY AND MAYO

On board the Connemara Lady

Views from the deck

Kayaking and watersports are popular here

Taking the plunge

KILLARY FJORD

Board the catamaran *Connemara Lady* at Nancy's Point pier, 2km west of Leenane village, and glide along Ireland's only glacial fjord enjoying some spectacular Connemara scenery. The Killary Fjord is 14km-long with a width ranging from 42 to 700m. On one side the landscape has ice age terraces in the form of Ordovician gritstones, shales and volcanic rocks, while the other has a special type of reef composed of Silurian sandstone and mudstone. Over the years this area has attracted many writers and artists to stay and work, among them Oscar Wilde and painter Paul Henry. During the voyage, a running commentary through loudspeakers (heard best on the outside decks) gives interesting details about the geology and history of the area. The *Connemara Lady*, owned by Killary Fjord Boat Tours, has excellent on-board facilities for 155 passengers, including inner decks, a dining space serving delicious seafood and a fully licensed bar. As the fjord is well sheltered, you can expect calm sailing conditions to generally apply. Highly recommended for a leisurely boat trip or for the more adventurous, kayaking and diving.

LETTERFRACK

Founded in 1849 by a Quaker family, the story of Letterfrack is a harrowing chapter in Irish history due to the horrific and tragic events that unfolded in St Joseph's Industrial School for boys from 1887, and up until it closed in 1974. The former Christian Brothers institution was plagued with physical and sexual abuse. A hillside graveyard in the village is littered with marble headstones commemorating seventy-nine named children who died while attending the industrial school. A visit to it can be a very moving experience. Post 1974, everything changed for the better in Letterfrack when members of the local community purchased the old school and a whole new era began. It now houses several excellent community--based projects. In 1980 the government established the Connemara National Park (see page 146), which unfurls beside the village – and Letterfrack was placed firmly on the tourist map. The village is home to an official Poetry Trail – one of only two in the West of Ireland. Poems are displayed on special plaques at different locations around the village. All were written by well-known Irish poets with the theme 'celebrating the importance of place'. Some are general in nature; others deal with the area's troubled history. A map is displayed in the Park Visitor Centre but one location is not revealed, inviting visitors to find the secret spot themselves. It's a poem written by the President of Ireland Michael D. Higgins. The drive to Letterfrack taking the N59 between Westport and Clifden is recommended for its stunning landscape. Along this route you can stop off at the exquisite Kylemore Abbey & Victorian Walled Garden.

The village is nestled beside Diamond Hill mountain

A scenic wonderland surrounds the village

A traditional thatched cottage

Poetic plaques are dotted around the Poetry Trail

The prettiest mountain streams

CONNEMARA NATIONAL PARK

The Connemara National Park covers a thin slice of the northwest sector of the Twelve Bens, stretching east as far as Benbrack, Bencullagh, Muckanaght and Benbaun. It includes an excellent walkway to the top of Diamond Hill (about 2hr 30min return). The path starts at the visitor centre and the 8km route follows the Sruffaunboy Nature Trail before branching off towards the cone of Diamond Hill. From the cairn on the summit ridge at 442m high the breathtaking view embraces islands, bays, beaches, loughs and mountains. There are three shorter nature trails across the lower slopes, through some natural woodland and over bogland, with free guided walks on Wednesday and Friday mornings in July and August. The park's visitor centre contains a fascinating exhibition on the wildlife and geology of Connemara and a café. There's also a children's playground. A trail map of the park is available to download from the website at www.connemaranationalpark.ie. From here you can easily take in Letterfrack on the same day (see page 144) for its lovely Poetry Trail.

Natural habitats for the park's flora and fauna abound

The park at dusk

Kilometres of hiking trails in stunning surroundings

Follow Irish legend and seek a pot of gold at the end of a rainbow

DOG'S BAY BEACH

Soft white sand on a sheltered horseshoe bay that stretches for 1.5km... Dog's Bay Beach in County Galway is one of the prettiest beaches in Ireland. Indeed, on a fine day you'd be forgiven for imagining you were far from the bracing bite of the Atlantic Ocean. The slim strip of dunes that separates it from Gurteen Beach has, as in many coastal areas, been planted with Marram grass in a bid to prevent coastal erosion. Take to the beach year-round for a walk or lay out the towels in summer. Swimming is possible here, too, but there are no lifeguards on duty so caution is advised. Afterwards, drive the short 2km to the lovely fishing village of Roundstone where you can dine in *O'Dowd's Seafood Bar and Restaurant*, enjoying the freshest catch of the day – think hake, haddock, mussels, crab and lobster; hearty chowder and meaty mains, all in a traditional Irish pub setting, perhaps accompanied by a pint of Guinness or a glass of wine.

Beach perfection in Galway

Delicious with a squeeze of lemon

GALWAY OYSTER FESTIVAL

The Galway Oyster Festival is one of Europe's longest-running food festivals and has been drawing people to County Galway for over 64 years. In that time it has been featured in *The Sunday Times*, *BBC Good Food*, and *Time* magazine, among others worldwide. So why are these oysters so celebrated? It's a debatable topic but some would say it is the perfect harvesting conditions that give them an unrivalled taste; a combination of the sheltered setting and the Atlantic mixed with the sweet notes derived from the limestone in the Burren and the smoky, peaty flavour of the Connemara bogs. The festival celebrates the first oyster harvest of the season with gusto, offering a programme of music, delicious seafood, cookery demos, parade, and of course, the Guinness World Oyster Opening Championship (each competitor must open thirty of the molluscs as quickly as possible and present them perfectly on a tray). Wash down your oysters with a pint of Guinness, the unofficial beverage of choice. Alternatively, there is no shortage of champagne, fine wine or indeed any other tipple of your choice. Not big on oysters? Don't worry. The atmosphere and *craic* alone make this one not to miss.

A lovely pairing - Guinness and oysters

An important announcement

The Oyster Opening Championship

Annual colourful festivities

INIS MÓR

The largest of the Aran Islands, Inis Mór is an otherworldly eruption of rugged limestone jutting out into the squalls and storms of the Atlantic, on the very western edge of Europe. This ancient land holds evidence of prehistoric habitation as far back as 3000 BC, and today remains home to 900 hardy and deeply Irish souls. While just forty minutes from the mainland by ferry, the farthest of these famous islands feels a world apart from – at times – Earth itself. The island's jagged coastlines, sea-scraped limestone plateaus and mysterious, ancient clifftop forts feel straight out of an interstellar sci-fi blockbuster or fantasy epic. Humans have a foothold on this island but will always share it with the sea and its creatures. The bizarre wormhole (known as the 'Serpent's Lair') is a naturally formed and almost perfectly rectangular pool sliced out of the base of the cliffs, seemingly carved by the hand of some ancient ocean god. Beware entering, however, as its waters are fed through underground caves and can drain in the blink of an eye — or suddenly rage with a great Atlantic swell. When you're ready to return to the human world you'll find warm hearths and fine food, away from the seals and seabirds, at a number of excellent pubs dotted around the island.

The rugged cliff-face

Uncrowded beaches are a given

Ancient fort

The Serpent's Lair

NEWPORT

Newport, a heritage town located on the shores of Clew Bay in County Mayo along the Wild Atlantic Way, has many interesting places to explore. The town's centrepiece is the Victorian red stone railway viaduct with seven arches (in operation from 1894-1937). There is also an abbey, ancient wood ringfort, plus the last stained-glass window designed by world-famous artist Harry Clarke in the local church. Another big attraction is seeing the ancestral home of actress Grace Kelly, later to become Princess Grace of Monaco. Grace Kelly's paternal grandfather was named John whose original home was a small thatched cottage a couple of kilometres from Newport. He emigrated to Philadelphia in 1887 where he founded a major construction company. As Princess Grace of Monaco, the former Hollywood star, made several visits to the town during the sixties and seventies, there are several photos of these visits in the local tourist information office. On her last stay she examined plans to build a holiday home on the original site. However, this never reached fruition as she died following a car accident a couple of years later. Newport has two hotels, Irish music pubs and several cafés. Be sure to drop into Kelly's artisan butchers' shop, winners of numerous awards for dry cured rashers, sausages and both black and white puddings.

The bridge into town

Perfect stargazing conditions

MAYO DARK SKY PARK

In 2016 the Mayo Dark Sky Park was officially launched following a submission sent to the International Dark-Sky Association based in Arizona and accepted. It was designated as Gold Tier, the highest possible accolade. There are just one hundred such parks around the world. As a follow up, it was decided to hold an annual festival here. If you enjoy looking at, or have a particular interest in, the night sky then the Mayo Dark Sky Festival held each November should be on your must-do list. While the festival takes place mainly around Wild Nephin National Park, several events over the weekend are held in neighbouring towns of Newport (see page 154) and Mulranny. There are always lots of activities such as torchlight walks, science workshops, a mobile planetarium and, of course, stargazing. Many well-known names in the fields of science and night sky photography regularly attend. However, any time of the year is good to visit this unspoilt region consisting of the Nephin Beg Range and Owenbeg bog, the last intact blanket bog system in Ireland and Western Europe. The Ballycroy Visitor Centre offers lots of information about the immediate area and upstairs is an excellent café.

Starry splendour

The aurora borealis

Stargazing from every spot

St Patrick's Church, Newport

Idyllic island accommodation

A room with a view

An inviting cycle trail

Explore the island by bike

CLARE ISLAND

Rugged and mountainous, Clare Island stands guard at the entry of Clew Bay. Always in sight from the shores of County Mayo and shrouded in mystery, this little land is home to the tomb of a pirate queen, numerous Bronze Age sites and old sailors' pubs frozen in time. Most travellers hop over on a daytrip before ploughing on through their packed itinerary, or bypass it altogether, but Clare Island will reward patient travellers who give it more of their time. It has an atmosphere of its own, sparsely populated and ringed with towering cliffs, but doesn't lack in golden-sanded beaches and peaceful woodlands. Claimed in the sixteenth century by the Ó Máille dynasty and its pirate queen, who controlled the seas of Connacht from this hardy outpost, it formed the perfect setting for Michael Morpurgo's award-winning children's novel, *The Ghost of Grania O'Malley*. Frequently clashing with the English Tudors and dispatching Spanish Armada sailors who washed up on the island's shore, 'Grannia O'Malley' and her kin carved out a fierce reputation that persists to this day. Get swept up in the legend of the pirate queen before arriving or while you're there, exploring the peaceful island and enjoying its fresh air with few other souls, if any, for company. A number of excellent holiday homes, including the majestic lighthouse itself, make it a great base for a true getaway.

KEEM BAY

A secluded beach hidden on an island, with golden sand and crystal blue water, ringed by green cliffs and offering incredible views? Not heaven, but almost. This one-of-a-kind spot is found on Achill Island, the largest isle in the country, which sits at one of the westernmost points of Europe. Catch Keem Bay on a sunny day and you could be forgiven for thinking you've stumbled across the Atlantic and into the Caribbean. The beach is located at the bottom of a deep, horseshoe bay, giving it great protection from the elements and a wonderful sense of seclusion. With a Blue Flag certification for cleanliness, the utterly clear waters here are perfect for taking in the marine life of the wild west coast by swimming, diving and snorkelling. It exerts its pull year-round, making it a great spot to soak up the summer sun or walk up onto the cliffs for dramatic views. Keem Bay is accessed just off the Wild Atlantic Way, requiring a jaw-dropping detour to reach. Taking a guided kayak tour of the island will give you a chance to explore the other stretches of coastline that Achill Island has to offer, well combined with fishing and a range of other watersports.

The idyllic bay

The prettiest bay

A soft sand beach

Achill Island sheep

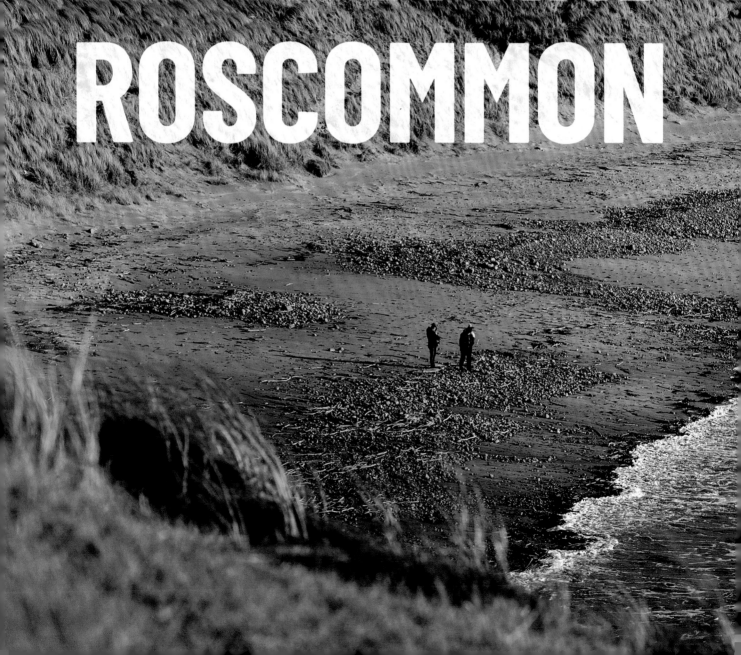

SLIGO, LEITRIM AND ROSCOMMON

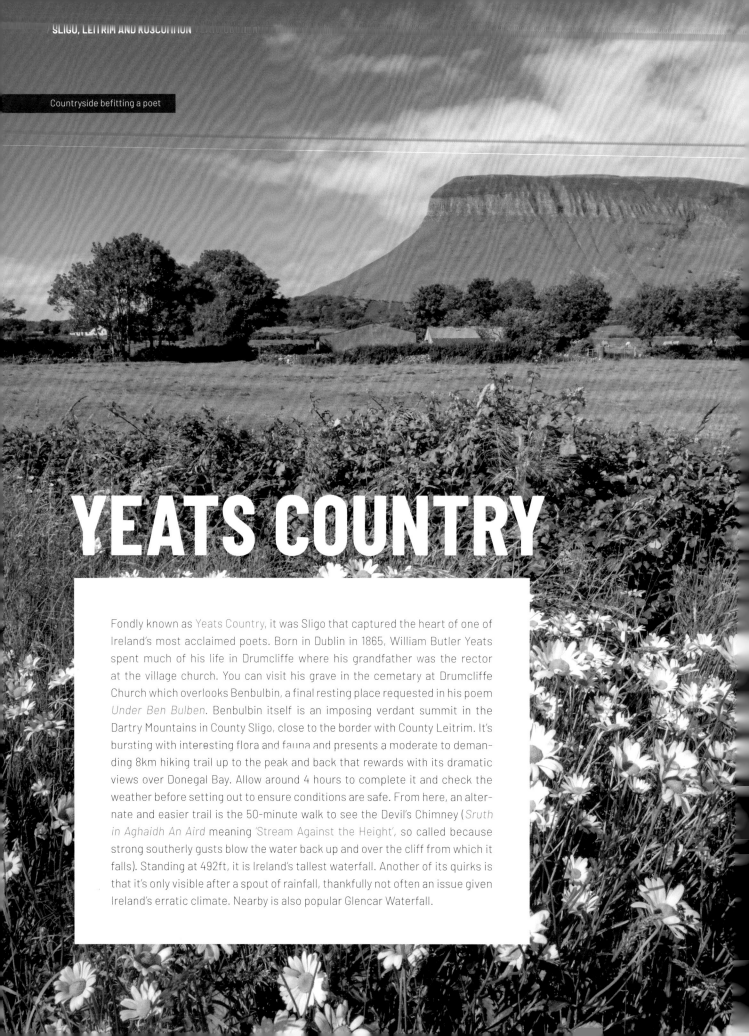

Countryside befitting a poet

YEATS COUNTRY

Fondly known as Yeats Country, it was Sligo that captured the heart of one of Ireland's most acclaimed poets. Born in Dublin in 1865, William Butler Yeats spent much of his life in Drumcliffe where his grandfather was the rector at the village church. You can visit his grave in the cemetary at Drumcliffe Church which overlooks Benbulbin, a final resting place requested in his poem *Under Ben Bulben*. Benbulbin itself is an imposing verdant summit in the Dartry Mountains in County Sligo, close to the border with County Leitrim. It's bursting with interesting flora and fauna and presents a moderate to demanding 8km hiking trail up to the peak and back that rewards with its dramatic views over Donegal Bay. Allow around 4 hours to complete it and check the weather before setting out to ensure conditions are safe. From here, an alternate and easier trail is the 50-minute walk to see the Devil's Chimney (*Sruth in Aghaidh An Aird* meaning 'Stream Against the Height', so called because strong southerly gusts blow the water back up and over the cliff from which it falls). Standing at 492ft, it is Ireland's tallest waterfall. Another of its quirks is that it's only visible after a spout of rainfall, thankfully not often an issue given Ireland's erratic climate. Nearby is also popular Glencar Waterfall.

Benbulbin's dramatic setting

W B Yeats' grave in Drumcliffe

The waterfall on a dry day

The Devil's Chimney waterfall

CONEY ISLAND

The original Coney Island, it was this sand-laced speck off Strandhill in County Sligo that gave its American counterpark its name, or so the story goes. Vastly different in appearance, there are no fairground attractions here, just a few kilometres of beach in an unspoilt location. Legend has it that the sea captain of a nineteenth-century merchant ship *Arethusa* who sailed the route from Sligo to New York, having taken note of the large number of rabbits in New York, decided to name the American neighbourhood after his own island off the Coolera peninsula in Sligo - the word 'Coney' coming from the Irish word *coinín* (pronounced *quin-neen*) for rabbit. A cute story, whether there is any truth to it or not. To get here you can hop on a boat from Rosses Point or follow the more fun driving route waymarked by fourteen stone pillars from Cummeen Strand for 5km - accessible at low tide only. Come spend a few hours on uncrowded, pristine beaches, enjoy a spot of surfing or a dip in the sea, then saunter in for a pint in the island's only pub, *McGowans*. Just make sure to time your return with the tide or you'll be stopping overnight.

RIVER SHANNON BLUEWAY

Turn off from the Wild Atlantic Way coast road and you'll find many paths less travelled throughout the country's lush interior. The River Shannon Blueway is one such network of biking and hiking trails, weaving around the many lakes, canals and rivers of Leitrim. A county that got its first traffic lights in 2016, it offers an excellent break from travelling by car. Leave the tourist tarmac and explore a number of unspoiled landscapes by foot and bike on land, or cruise the waterways by kayak, canoe or stand-up paddleboard. Dotted with excellent restaurants and up-and-coming gastropubs, the Shannon Blueway's well-fed travellers can glide through nearly 50km of fields, forests and fallen ruins from Drumshanbo to the tip of Lough Ree. Complete the whole trail from end to end if you're feeling adventurous, or just rock up to any of the many entry points for a short walking loop, guided paddle, or just to relax by the water. A host of quaint villages and waterside towns will greet you along your travels, each suffused with its own unique blend of raucous pubs and fine dining options, musical communities, historical oddities and plenty of 'Decent People' — as residents of Leitrim are nicknamed.

Kayaking on the Blueway

Riverside dining in Carrick-on-Shannon

Shannon boat tours are a great way to explore

Woodland walking trails

Comfy beds ensure a good night's sleep

The popular Hobbit House

The glamping yurts

Inside the Hobbit House

PINK APPLE ORCHARD

Situated at the top of the beautiful Lough Allen in the Glens of North Leitrim, Pink Apple Orchard's nature-focused glamping site should be top of your list if you want to get away from it all. Spread out across a cider apple orchard are three handmade Celtic yurts, the Hobbit House and gypsy wagon, all within their own private space. The Hobbit House is gorgeous, and the most luxurious of the accommodation options, with electricity, a woodburning stove and private bathroom. It has a grass-covered roof and a circular entrance with a beautiful wooden door. The communal kitchen is well kitted out with everything you need for self-catering, as well as books and games for any rainy days, while just outside is a large communal barbecue area with views of the lough and the Iron mountains. The yurts feature small woodburning stoves and furniture which is handmade onsite, and just outside each is a small seating area. The Johnson family have clearly put their heart and soul into their business, with an attention to detail and passion for nature which will really enhance your stay in this tranquil part of Ireland.

The Honey Badger Bar

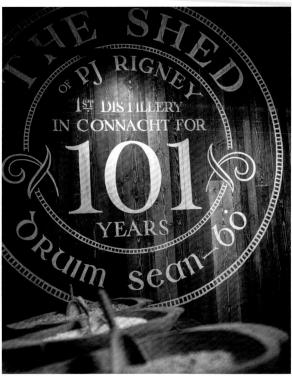

The distillery has a long history

The gin comes in pretty coloured bottles

The Jackalope Café

THE SHED DISTILLERY

Gin glorious gin, in pretty bottles, too. The Shed Distillery first began its journey in 2014, a mere 101 years after whiskey was last distilled in the province of Connacht. Using copper pot and column stills, PJ Rigney's vision was to create exceptional drinks using age-old, traditional methods. Set by the shores of Lough Allen and at the foot of the Iron Mountain, the setting is spectacular too. Come early and enjoy breakfast or lunch in the Jackalope Café before embarking on a tour. Tastings are of the Drumshanbo Still Irish Pot Whiskey as well as the Gunpowder Irish Gin. Keen to let the experience linger? Stop by the shop and bring your favourite tipple home.

The entrance to the distillery

ARIGNA MINES

Arigna was Ireland's last working coal mine, in use from the 1700s to the 1990s. Located amid the beautiful scenery of Lough Allen, the surrounding land was not well suited to agriculture and so coal mining provided a valuable income for local people. The mine has been impressively repurposed with strong local community support into a valuable and fascinating insight into the working lives of miners, while the unique visitor centre was designed to resemble a coal slag heap. Tours into the mine are run by ex-miners who provide a wealth of first-hand knowledge and experience. The exhibition area features historical documents, photographs and early mining equipment, bringing to life nearly four hundred years of mining history. A short film also captures footage of mining taking place just before the closure of the mine. Following your visit, you could stretch your legs by taking a walk along the Miner's Way and Historical trail, a 118km-long network of paths stretching into Roscommon's neighbouring counties of Leitrim and Sligo. Then quench your thirst in the Miners Bar in Arigna, which has a beer garden overlooking the river, or if the weather is not so obliging, an open fire for a cosy pint or two.

The mines

Heading deeper into the mine

Waymarked trails are easy to follow

Machinery used for mining

One of the mounds

Informative panels in the Visitor Centre

Ghoulish displays tell the story of the site

Inside Oweynagat Cave - the 'Gates of Hell'

RATHCROGHAN

Although it is one of the most important historical and mythological sites in Ireland, Rathcroghan in County Roscommon is often overlooked in favour of more developed attractions. The complex encompasses hundreds of archaeological sites including ringforts, burial mounds and standing stones, spanning 5500 years of human history. It was the home of Medb, Queen of Connacht, and is an integral part of the Táin Bó Cúailnge epic. The sites are largely unexcavated, and many are located on private land, therefore a tour run by the Rathcroghan Visitor Centre is highly recommended. The tour provides valuable interpretation of the landscape, the guides being knowledgeable and passionate about their subject. This will also include a visit to the evocative Oweynagat Cave, entrance to 'the Underworld' or the 'Gates of Hell', and origin of the Halloween traditions of today. You can choose to go into the cave but you will almost certainly get muddy so don't wear your best clothes for this trip. The cave is part natural feature and partly altered by man over time, and features Ogham stones at the entrance. Legend has it that during Samhain (the festival marking the beginning of winter and starting on October 31) the underworld would open and all manner of beasts and monsters could enter the world of the living. In order to protect themselves, local people would dress in ghoulish disguises to fool the demons, thus the tradition of dressing up for Halloween.

RINDOON MEDIEVAL TOWN

On the Warrenpoint peninsula lies the deserted medieval town of Rindoon, regarded as an unparalleled set of ruins, and yet almost entirely undisturbed since its abandonment centuries ago. The Norman-era ruins include a town wall, castle, hospital, church and mill. This has not been developed into a tourist attraction, there is no visitor centre, and your only company will most likely be some grazing cattle. This belies the fact that at its most populous the town was home to around one thosuand people. A looped walk will take you around the peninsula, taking in beautiful views across Lough Ree. A short stroll away, on the western shores of Lough Ree near the village of Lecarrow, St John's Wood is one of Ireland's largest surviving ancient woodlands, an incredibly valuable habitat and a reminder of what much of the landscape would have looked like before massive deforestation. It forms part of Lough Ree Special Area of Conservation. The wood's age and lack of disturbance has led to wonderful biodiversity, providing shelter to pine martens, wood warblers and flowers such as the bird's-nest orchid. The wild cherry tree is also particularly common in this wood, and you can see fabulous swathes of bluebells during the spring.

The remains of Rindoon

Displays inside the musuem

The opulent dining room

The National Famine Museum

Pottery pieces that have stood the test of time

STROKESTOWN HOUSE

An impressive Palladian mansion, Strokestown House was owned by the same family (the Mahons) for over three hundred years. Now in the care of the Irish Heritage Trust, it is best known for housing the National Famine Museum which details both the local history of the Park's aristocratic landlords and their tenants, as well as the larger national factors which contributed to the Great Irish Famine in the mid-nineteenth century. The house itself is a beautiful example of Georgian architecture and the tour provides a fascinating insight into the lives of the gentry and servants, as not only are the grand rooms open to view, but also the kitchens and servants' quarters. Outside are six acres of walled gardens which include one of Ireland's longest herbaceous borders, a fernery and a Victorian rose garden. The surrounding woodland offers family-friendly trails and a number of ancient beech and oak trees planted by the original owners of the estate. Original garden machinery is on display and a refurbished glasshouse gives a glimpse into how the estate gardens were managed to provide food for the 'big house'. The National Famine Museum is regarded as the foremost educational resource on the subject in the country. Enjoy state-of-the-art multimedia exhibitions, touchscreen facilities and a presentation of priceless original documents hidden away for more than half a century which give a dramatic account of the living conditions of tenants, labourers and landlords. Walking around the impressive building, a vivid picture emerges of the parallel lives of rich and poor during that dreadful period in Irish history. A museum ticket also allows access to the walled gardens and woodland walk. Leave time for a snack in the spacious bright new café in the old granary.

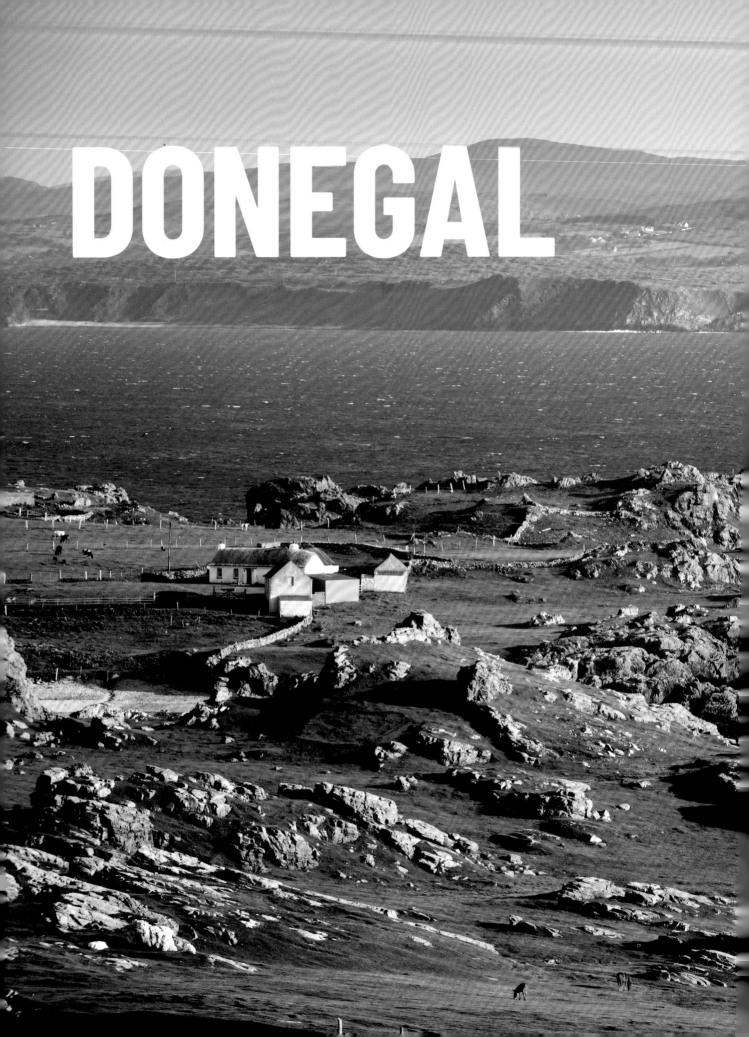

DONEGAL

The dramatic Atlantic coastline

Idyllic sailing waters

A beach worthy of the trip to get to it

The remains of the signal tower

MALIN HEAD

The northernmost outpost of Ireland, Malin Head is the Republic at its most elemental, an exhilaratingly remote landscape providing respite from the white noise of modernity. On offer are beautiful beaches and mighty sand dunes, gusty clifftop walks, and premier-class flora and fauna. Birding is big news here, with a healthy population of choughs populating the cliffs, while between October and March, the fields teem with thousands of Greenland barnacle geese chomping incessantly off the rich pasture, packing away enough to provide them with sufficient energy for the 2000-mile return journey; here, too, you might even hear the rasping cry of the elusive corncrake. Check out the view from Banba's Crown, a storm-lashed promontory named for a mythological goddess and topped by a ruined Napoleonic signal tower, from where a path heads out to Hell's Hole, a 75m chasm in the cliffs pounded by the onrushing tide. From the Head's many blustery vantage points, there are some fine vistas, including Fanad Head Lighthouse and Tory Island to the west, and – once the massed ranks of clouds have dispersed – the Scottish island of Islay over to the northwest. Get your timings right and you may even catch a glimpse of the Northern Lights. And where better to kick back with a pint of the black stuff than in Ireland's northernmost pub, Farren's Bar, as convivial a joint as anywhere in the country.

One Man's Pass

SLIEVE LEAGUE

A magical masterpiece of nature, the Slieve League (*Sliabh Liag*) – one of the most spectacular sections of the Wild Atlantic Way, a coastal strip that runs for 1600 miles along Ireland's western seaboard – remains a relatively little-visited part of the Republic. This is somewhat surprising given that these are the highest accessible sea cliffs in Ireland and some of the highest anywhere in Europe, standing at a whopping 1972ft or double the height of the Eiffel Tower. The Slieve serves up some terrific walks, from the easy – such as the 45-minute trek from the upper car park to the Bunglass Point viewpoint – to the short but tough Pilgrim's Path, an outing really only suited to seasoned hikers. Those with a head for heights might like to test their mettle on its extension, the One Man's Pass (the clue is in the name), a thrilling, knife-edge walk along a stony track high above the Atlantic. Reaching the summit of Slieve League, you'll be rewarded with an outlook as memorable as anywhere else on the Emerald Isle. Keep a close eye on the weather too – not so much because of the rain, but rather the heavy mists that frequently roll in from the Atlantic. But if you do make it up here, and get the views to boot, then you really are in for a treat and a half.

The narrow hiking trail

Boat trips are an alternate way to see the sights

The best views reward those who hike the trail

A natural outdoor playground for the intrepid

Quaint island houses

The lighthouse

Unspoilt beauty

Welcome to Tory Island

TORY ISLAND

Buffeted by seething Atlantic waves nine miles off the northwest coast of Donegal, Tory Island is Ireland's remotest inhabited island. Small it may be, but the island and its Gaelic-speaking residents – all 150 of them squeezed onto a wedge of rock just three miles by one – is thriving; it's now even got its own school. A resilient and welcoming bunch, Tory Islanders will guarantee first-class hospitality to any visitor, which extends to opening the doors to all-comers for evenings of Gaelic storytelling and *ceilidhs*, held all year round. Not that Tory's residents are particularly inclined to making concessions to modern-day visitors' busy timetables – you have been warned... Above all else, the island is renowned for its primitive, or naïve, landscape painters, a small coterie of artists who emerged in the 1960s, led by the English painter Derek Hill. The latter went on to influence the likes of James Dixon, a crofter and fisherman whose former home is now a gallery where a small but fascinating record of Tory Island life over fifty years is beautifully documented.

GLENVEAGH CASTLE

Glenveagh Castle was built on a small promontory for wealthy landowner George Adair between 1870 and 1873. The rhododendron-filled gardens surrounding the castle were very much the work of Adair's wife, Cornelia, who also introduced herds of red deer to the estate. The steep ascent to the viewpoint behind the gardens is more than worthwhile for the wonderful views down to the castle and along the lough deep into the glen in Glenveagh National Park. The Poisoned Glen - east of Dunlewey Lough, is one of the most popular spots of the park. Overall, it's easy to imagine why the castle was so popular during the Golden Age of Hollywood, with Greta Garbo, Marilyn Monroe and Clark Gable all spending time here. Guided tours of the castle focus on the furniture and artwork collected by the millionaire Irish-American, Henry McIlhenny, the last owner of Glenveagh. The Glenveagh National Park Visitor Centre has detailed and interactive displays on the area's ecology and geology. More interesting is the exhibition on the park's wildlife, and in particular its eagles. Minibuses will shuttle you back and forth to the castle from here.

Dunlewey Lough

Grand interiors

The castle

Aerial view of the castle and its gardens

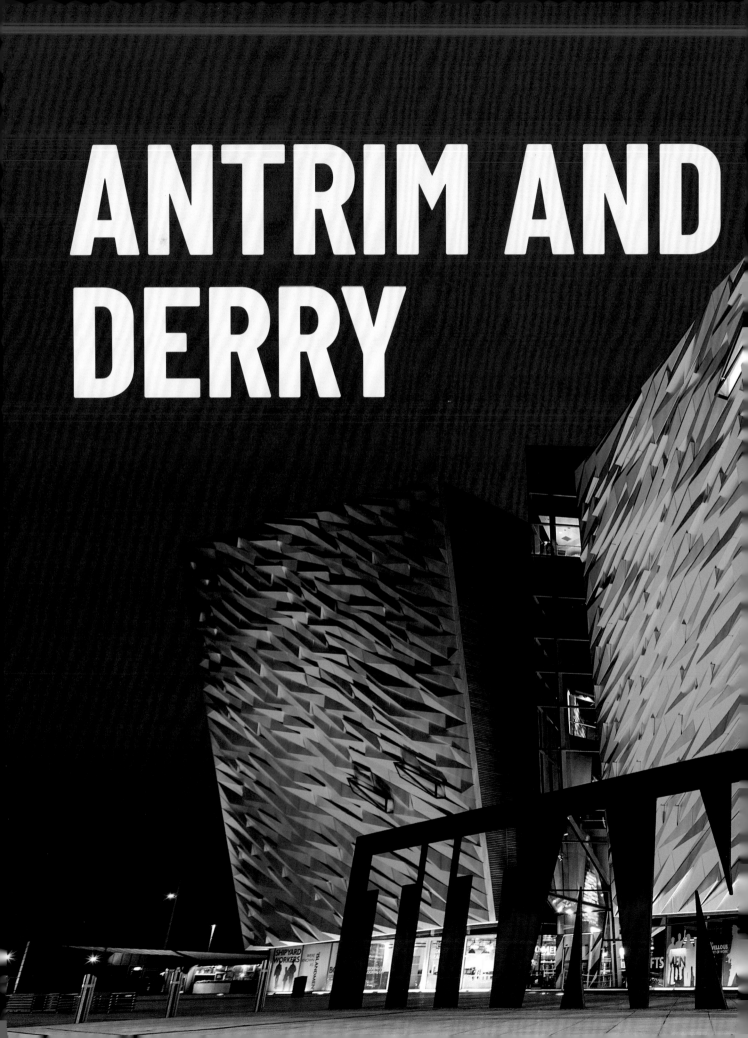

ANTRIM AND DERRY

Live music in *Fibber McGee's*

THE LINEN QUARTER

Belfast's emergence as a bona fide tourist destination owes much to the regeneration of the Linen Quarter, so-named from the time when Belfast could lay fair claim to being the linen capital of the world, an industry that played a pivotal role in the city's social and economic development during the nineteenth century. Many of the quarter's distinctive red brick warehouses remain, one of which is now the Linen Hall Library, the oldest in Belfast and whose archives are second to none. Peruse, too, the display of political posters as you head up the stairwell towards the café. Worth investigating also is the Linen Quarter's musical heritage, whether it's a performance at the prestigious Grand Opera House, a classical soirée at the Ulster Hall (Charles Dickens once read here) or some head-throbbing rock at the legendary *Limelight* club; not forgetting, either, *Fibber McGee's*, which hosts Irish music seven days a week. Last word, however, goes to *The Crown Liquor Saloon* (see page 196), a timeless Victorian gin palace that is emphatically one not to be missed.

The Buena Vista Social Club performing at Ulster Hall

Aerial view of Belfast

The Grand Opera House

Linen Hall Library

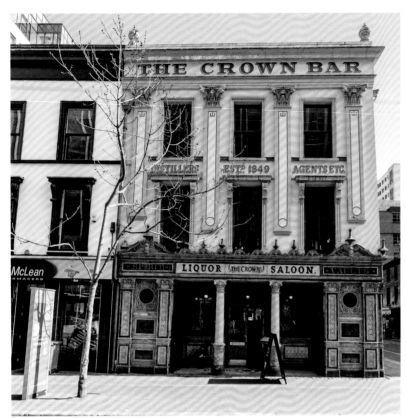

The stunning facade

At the bar

Expert pint pulling

The lavish Victorian exterior

THE CROWN LIQUOR SALOON

Taking pride of place in the very centre of Belfast, this perfectly preserved and opulent Victorian 'gin palace' offers a drinking experience like no other. *The Crown Liquor Saloon* has changed hands many times over the years, but its exquisite features remain frozen in time since the nineteenth century. Italian craftsmen working on local churches were directed towards the creation of an alternative place of solace, comfort and beauty in the 1880s. A lavish drinking establishment, fit for its fashionable patrons, emerged in a riot of kaleidoscopic tiles, stained-glass and ornate wood panelling. Today you'll find a chance to tip back a glass in much the same way customers have been for over a hundred years. Heated footrests sit underneath a massive granite-topped bar studded with brass taps, imposing ale casks and Neoclassical wooden columns, while ten private booths with latched doors allow the drinkers of today and yesteryear to imbibe away from prying eyes. Take a seat in one and you'll find gunmetal panels for striking matches and antique ringing bells for summoning (non-antique) bar staff. Your eyes will never tire in here, drinking in the mosaic floors and delicate carved ceilings until a plate of hearty Irish pub fare arrives in front of you.

A memorial to Bobby Sands

EVERYONE, REPUBLICAN OR OTHERWISE HAD THEIR OWN PARTICULAR ROLE TO PLAY

...OUR REVENGE WILL BE THE LAUGHTER OF OUR CHILDREN

Bobby Sands MP

POET, GAEILGEOIR, REVOLUTIONARY, IRA VOLUNTEER

BELFAST POLITICAL TOUR

The Troubles is a definitive period in Northern Irish history. This conflict – a war to some – drew its fuel across nationality, politics and religion, plaguing the country and its neighbours for several decades. There are few residents of Belfast who haven't been impacted by it in some way; its scars are visible to this day, with 26km of peace walls still dividing neighbourhoods and many locals living with broken families, friends lost or painful memories. The Belfast Political Tour (www.belfastpoliticaltour.com) is a chance to move beyond the page of history or documentary screen, getting a real glimpse into this turbulent period and the stories of those involved. Led and delivered by ex-political prisoners from both sides of the divide, they'll let you see through their eyes and feel what they felt as they risked imprisonment, injury or death for their beliefs. Weaving through the streets and landmarks of the city, it's an undeniably unique and visceral, immediate experience. One guide will pass you over to another through a gate in the peace wall at the tour's mid-point, tactfully combining the history and humanity of what is still recent, raw and not entirely resolved for the people of Belfast.

Hole in the wall mural

The tour at the International Wall

The tour on Bombay Street

Falls Road murals

TITANIC QUARTER

History famously recollects that the *RMS Titanic* was built here at the Harland & Wolff shipyard in east Belfast between 1909 and 1912, and sank just four days into her maiden voyage, on 12 April 1912. It's a story that is memorably recalled in Titanic Belfast, the centrepiece of the Titanic Quarter, one of Europe's largest urban waterfront regeneration projects. A stunning prow-like structure (at 38m – the same height as the ship's hull) clad with some three thousand silver-anodised aluminium shards, it's an inspiring testament to both the doomed ship and the city that built it, a fully immersive exhibition that propels visitors back to the early twentieth century. The highlight is a shipyard experience ride that sees passengers travel through the sights and sounds of Harland & Wolff as it circumnavigates a replica of the ship's rudder during construction. The *Titanic* herself may only be present in spirit, but her tender ship, the *SS Nomadic*, is permanently moored in Hamilton Dock; it's the last remaining White Star Line vessel in the world. There's more to the Titanic Quarter than just big ships, though: it's home to the *Game of Thrones* trail, a series of stained-glass installations dotted along the Maritime Mile, shops, restaurants and bars, and the massive SSE Arena.

The Titanic Quarter

The exhibition hall at Titanic Belfast

SS Nomadic

One of the lifeboats from *RMS Titanic*

The stone columns up close

Former fortresses

The causeway juts into the sea

Carrick-a-Rede rope bridge

GIANT'S CAUSEWAY

Some say that it was the legendary Irish giant Fionn mac Cumhall (or Fin McCool) who carved out the Giant's Causeway in order to reach Scotland to fight his Celtic nemesis Benandonner. Others maintain that it was Bernandonner himself who built the walkway before tearing it up as he fled in terror after being tricked into mistaking the disguised Fionn for his giant baby son – nice stories both, but the more prosaic reality was that this marvel of nature was formed as a result of a volcanic eruption some sixty million years ago, which left the molten basalt to cool into the remarkable rock formations we see today: some 40,000 upright hexagonal basalt columns standing like soldiers on sentry. As Northern Ireland's classic travel icon – and the sole Unesco World Heritage Site – the Causeway constantly bristles with visitors, but there are ways to avoid the hordes. The catch is, you'll have to walk there (though by doing so you avoid the expensive car park fee), which is no hardship, especially if you approach it along the Causeway Coast Way which stretches for some 51km between Ballycastle in the east to Portstewart in the west. Highlights en route include Dunluce Castle, the vertigo-inducing Carrick-a-Rede rope bridge, and a wee stop at The Bushmills Inn, whose whiskey has been distilled there since 1608, giving it the proud distinction of being the world's oldest licenced distillery. Its inn, complete with rooms, restaurant and bar is top draw too.

THE GOBBINS

Chiselled into the base of a cliff face on the eastern flank of the long, banana-shaped Islandmagee peninsula, The Gobbins is an unforgettable 3km-long walkway tracing the Atlantic coastline. Derived from the Gaelic *gobán*, meaning 'headland', the Gobbins was originally conceived by railway engineer and one man tourist board, Berkeley Deane Wise, in 1902 in an attempt to lure a new class of Edwardian visitor to the area. Eventually closed in 1960, it reopened in 2015. Following a short safety briefing – it's by no means a dangerous or taxing trek, but a reasonable level of fitness and a moderate head for heights is desirable. Kitted out with hardhat, you're bussed down to the start of the path which begins at a viewing point affording tremendous views of the sea-bitten coastline and in the distance the faint hump of Ailsa Craig just off the Ayrshire coast. The walk proper begins at Wise's Eye, a diminutive tunnel bored into the rock face; thereafter, the new 3km-long path roughly tracks Wise's original, albeit now almost totally eroded, version, running through a series of dramatic tunnels, staircases and suspension bridges, including a replica of Wise's iconic tubular bridge. The birdlife here is first-class too: kittiwakes, guillemots, razorbills and puffins cling precariously to the cliff ledges, while gannets spear headfirst into the North Channel's foamy waters in frenzied pursuit of mackerel.

A dramatic walkway

An adrenaline-fuelled walk above the Atlantic

The Gobbins cliff path

Guillemots perched on the rock face

Razorbills nestled in a craggy nook

An island viewing point

Island residents

Have a pint of the black stuff in *McCuaigs*

Rathlin West Lighthouse, a beacon for ships on a foggy night

RATHLIN ISLAND

Almost as close to the Mull of Kintyre in Scotland as it is to Ballycastle on the Irish mainland, the boot-shaped Rathlin Island is Northern Ireland's only inhabited island, yet despite its proximity to the mainland, Rathlin feels gloriously remote. It's a wild, craggy place with a coastline consisting almost entirely of limestone and basalt cliffs that rise some 200ft out of the Atlantic, and fields sheathed in blankets of wild orchids and banks of primroses. Rathlin offers much by way of real escape, not least outstanding birdlife, being home to one of the largest seabird colonies in Ireland, including fulmars, guillemots, razorbills and gannets, numbers swollen in spring by thousands of puffins. Factor in some terrific hiking and biking, locally caught seafood in the *Manor House* hotel, and creamy pints of Guinness and traditional music in *McCuaig's Bar*, and you're all set. Legend and lore swirl around Rathlin, much like the salty winds that batter the shoreline. The most famous of these has it that Robert the Bruce retreated to a cave here following defeat by the English at Perth, but seeing a spider determinedly trying to spin its web gave him the resolve to 'try, try and try again', and so it was that he returned to Scotland and defeated the English at Bannockburn. A great time to visit is the end of May for the Rathlin Sound Maritime Festival, a week-long jamboree of nautically themed events, the highlight of which is most likely to be the Blessing of the Boats ceremony.

View over Carnlough

Bedrooms are inviting with crisp linens

The whiskey bar

Tasty desserts on the menu

LONDONDERRY ARMS

Roughly halfway along the Causeway Coastal Route, in the comely seaside village of Carnlough, stands a lovely old hotel built in 1848 as a coaching inn by the Marchioness of Londonderry, and was later briefly owned by her descendant, Winston Churchill. Painted in a smart black-and-white palette, the *Londonderry Arms* oozes Georgian splendour, from the smart public areas to the warren of agreeably old-fashioned rooms variously conferred with carved oak and antique furnishings – and yes, you can stay in the one Churchill slept in; number 114 as it goes. The most enjoyable aspect of the hotel is the *Arkle Whiskey Bar*, named in honour of the legendary 1960s champion steeplechaser whose shoe from his victory in the 1965 Cheltenham Gold Cup is proudly mounted on the wall. This timeworn bar brims with villagey atmos-phere thanks to a merry band of loyal locals, an aromatic turf fire, and yellowed photographs and newspaper clip-pings all over the place. The hotel is the perfect spot from which to strike out into the Glens of Antrim, nine deeply incised valleys that radiate down from the Antrim Plateau towards the coast, or to pay a visit to the magnificent walled garden at Glenarm Castle. Alternatively, seek out the multitude of *Game of Thrones* locations in the area, the hugely popular fantasy series that has done more to boost Antrim's tourist trade than any marketing campaign could possibly ever hope to achieve.

The inn

PORTSTEWART STRAND

A glorious 3km stretch of sand firm enough to drive on – which many folk do – the National Trust-owned Portstewart Strand is so wide that you never feel crowded out. For the more active-minded, there's a terrific, and fairly easy, four-mile walk beginning at the Portstewart Visitor Centre, which takes you through age-old dunes dusted with tufts of pale green grasses, then down to the Bann estuary, where the path follows the river's edge and returns to the golden beach. Portstewart also offers some of the best surfing in the country: operating out of a van at the entrance to the car park, the friendly folk at *Ocean Warriors* will see to all your needs. Whilst here it'd be remiss not to pay a visit to *Harry's Shack*, a cool restaurant in a weathered, wood-panelled building occupying a low bluff at the edge of the dunes. Its wide-framed seascapes make for a captivating setting in which to indulge in gut-busting burgers and mounds of fresh seafood, including cones of spiced whitebait with Marie Rose sauce. But if it's just a taste of old-fashioned seaside fun you're after, make for *Morelli's*, a fabled *gelato* parlour that has been doling out heavenly sundaes since 1927.

The wide expanse that is Portstewart Strand

SEAMUS HEANEY HOMEPLACE

But I've no spade to follow men like them.
Between my finger and my thumb
The squat pen rests.
I'll dig with it.

Seamus Heaney, by common consensus Ireland's greatest contemporary poet was born in Bellaghy, an old plantation settlement near Lough Beg, in 1939. The closing lines of one of his first poems *Digging* captures his memories of his father digging potatoes and his grandfather digging turf as the poet puts pen to paper, all of them diligent workers in their own craft. Whether you're a fan of the late Nobel laureate and his work or not, the marvellous Seamus Heaney HomePlace is a fitting tribute to the man and makes for an interesting day out. Reposed within the village's old police station, but now sporting a handsome stone and wood clad exterior, HomePlace is run through with Heaney's words and spirit, from the audios of the poet himself reading his poems to the trove of personal effects, such as his black leather satchel and the duffel coat he wore as a young boy. Heaney is buried in the churchyard a few hundred metres from Homeplace, his simple grey headstone bearing the inscription *'Walk on air against your better judgement'*, a line from his poem *The Gravel Walks*.

Imagery reflecting his works

Personal effects belonging to the poet are on display

HomePlace

Words from Heaney's poetry

A place to sit and reflect

Outdoor tables on a fine day

The unassuming exterior

Pretty murals

A haven in the city

GARDEN OF REFLECTION

On every visit to Derry/Londonderry you are bound to discover a new place to explore. In recent years Derry has emerged as a vibrant city, attracting more and more tourists as time goes on. On every visitor's list are of course the Guildhall, stunning Peace Bridge over the River Foyle, Tower Museum and Museum of Free Derry situated in the Bogside, a name which became synonymous with Derry during The Troubles. But one special place to see is the Garden of Reflection in the heart of the city centre on Bishop Street. A peaceful small outdoor area used occasionally for civic events. It is described locally as a place for contemplation, which sums up this intimate urban space perfectly. Come here to enjoy the quirky street sculptures, small fountains and unusual pavement designs. The garden was somewhat aptly funded by the PEACE III Programme as part of the EU Regional Development Fund.

The riotous *Derry Girls*

The Museum of Free Derry

The murals evoke the pain of The Troubles

The artworks are a stark reminder of the recent past

THE BOGSIDE MURALS

Few places in Northern Ireland suffered as much during The Troubles as Derry, but to wander the streets today is to experience a city rejuvenated and, to an extent, reconciled, as symbolised by the Peace Bridge which snakes its way across the Foyle linking the largely Unionist community on the east bank with the majority Nationalist community on the west bank. The most tangible reminder of The Troubles are The Bogside Murals, a series of large-scale paintings curated by a triumvirate of local artists in the 1990s. Whilst not affiliated to any political group, the murals remain divisive, a stark reminder of the violence that tore the city apart. But by the same token, they have become a major tourist attraction. Among the more striking images are those of a gas-mask-clad petrol bomber, and another entitled the *Death of Innocence*, which commemorates a 14-year-old girl, Annette McGavigan, caught in crossfire between the British Army and IRA. The murals have spawned further recent works of street art, such as *The Derry Girls*, a vast canvas near the Foyleside Shopping Centre depicting the cast of the popular comedy series. For more insight into The Troubles, make a beeline for the Museum of Free Derry, which recalls the Bogside's traumatic history in compelling, and unavoidably harrowing, fashion; among the exhibits are some blood-soaked and bullet-pierced items of clothing of some of the victims.

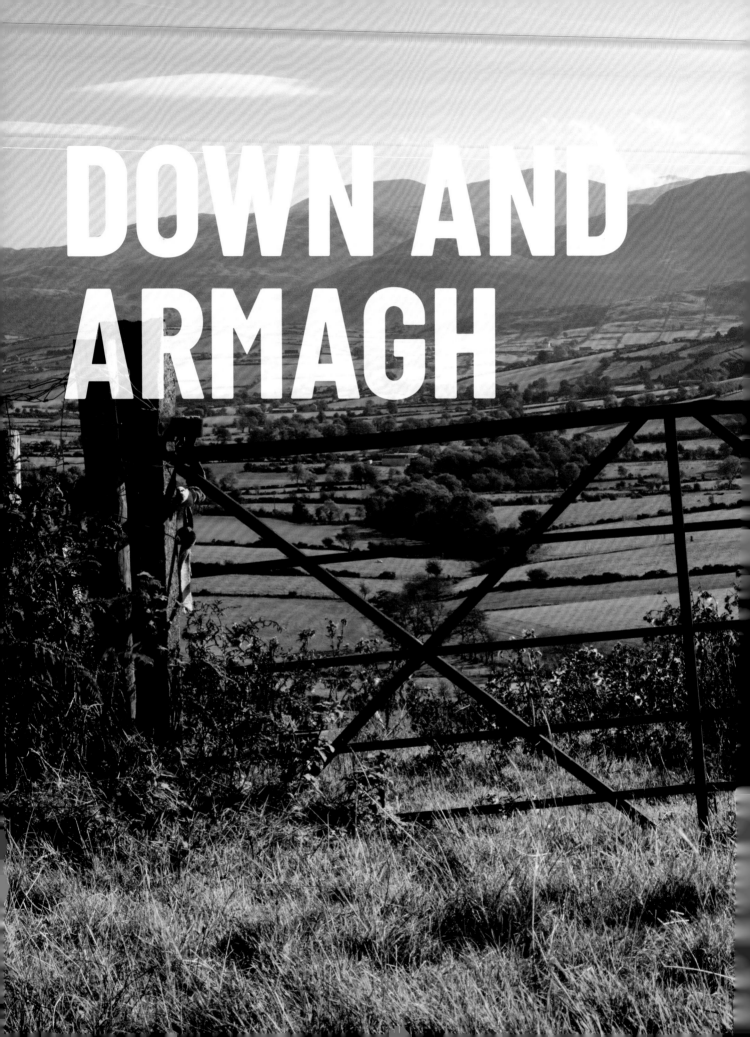

DOWN AND ARMAGH

MOUNT STEWART

Dramatically edging the western shore of Strangford Lough on the long and narrow Ards Peninsula stands Mount Stewart, the magnificent ancestral home of the Londonderry family. As entertaining as the guided tours of the house are – among the eccentric furnishings is a pair of hooves, now fashioned into inkwells, which belonged to Fighting Charlie, winner of the 1965 Ascot Gold Cup and ridden by the late, great Lester Piggott – it's the gardens that really enthral. Among the finest in all of Ireland, they were laid out in the 1920s by Edith, Marchioness of Londonderry, who was one serious horticulturalist, as well as a heavyweight society hostess and a pioneer pilot. Edith curated Italian and Spanish planting schemes, a funky shamrock garden complete with topiary harp, lake walks and lily woods, and a sea garden with date palms and rhododendrons to keep at bay the salt winds off the tidal lough. Craziest of all is the Dodo Terrace, flaunting various bits of giant statuary including the irritable-looking creatures themselves. Both Edith and her husband – the 7th Marquess of Londonderry – lie buried in an elaborate sarcophagi within the walled mausoleum, *Tír na nÓg*, high above the lake.

The Sunken Garden

Tir na nÓg

The Dodo Terrace

Autumn colour

Icy winter peaks

Hikers setting out

The deceptive peaks of the Mournes from afar

The Slieve Donard walk

MOURNE MOUNTAINS

For centuries, the Mourne Mountains have inspired writers, musicians and adventurers, from Percy French's songs to C.S Lewis's *Chronicles of Narnia*. More recently, it has been the television titan that is the *Game of Thrones*, much of which was filmed around these mountains – that has succeeded in establishing the Mournes as Northern Ireland's most valuable tourist draw. The Mournes are a relatively youthful set of granite mountains, with steep sides, moraines and occasional sheer cliffs, which gives them their sharp, jagged outline, but from a distance they appear much gentler, like a sleeping herd of buffalo. This is a truly ancient land, liberally sprinkled with prehistoric cairns and stone graves, many of which are said to mark the resting place of Irish chiefs. Set your hiking sights high with a yomp to the top of Slieve Donard (850m), Northern Ireland's highest peak and a steady five- to six-hour round trip, which begins from Donard Park, just a few minutes from the centre of the popular and agreeably cheerful seaside resort of Newcastle. Whilst hardly a colossus, the heather-softened flanks of this magical mountain remains a significant proposition and it is not to be taken lightly, especially given the notoriously unpredictable local weather. But once at the summit, on a clear day you are rewarded with peerless views over the Irish Sea towards the Isle of Man and the coastlines of Wales and Scotland.

ARMAGH CITY

While Belfast and Derry invariably receive all the accolades (and not unreasonably so), Armagh barely registers on most people's itineraries. More fool them, because this fine, big-hearted city simply begs to be explored. Begin with the city's twin ecclesiastical behemoths: the double-spired St Patrick's Church of Ireland Cathedral where, it is claimed, St Patrick founded his first church in 445AD – hence for many this is where the roots of Ireland lay – and, less than half a mile away on a neighbouring hill, St Patrick's Roman Catholic Cathedral, worth a lingering peek for its glittering wall-to-wall mosaics. Church sightseeing done, head down to The Mall, a vast and elegant oval green (it was once a racecourse) flanked by tree-lined promenades and rows of terraced Georgian houses. The city's real gem is the Armagh Robinson Library, which is not only the oldest library in all of Ireland but it also holds an extremely rare first edition of *Gulliver's Travels* annotated by Swift himself when he was Dean of the Anglican cathedral, as well as an early copy of Handel's *Messiah*; call ahead to visit. An easy local excursion is Navan Fort, home to the country's finest Iron Age legends and whose hill sites are exclusive to Ireland.

The city at sunset

The Mall

Navan Fort

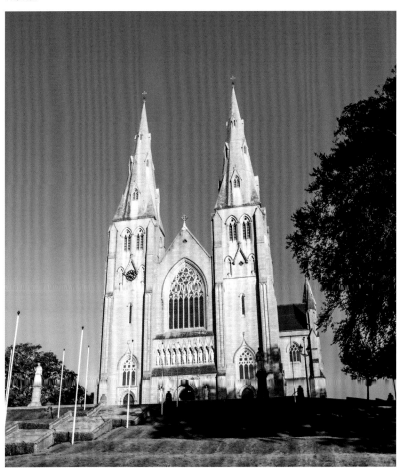

St Patrick's Church of Ireland Cathedral

Splendid Georgian architecture

The vast volcanic landscape around the Ring of Gullion

RING OF GULLION

An eerily volcanic landscape marking the border with County Louth in south Armagh, the Ring of Gullion (1991) and has the honour of being the first ring dyke in the world to be geologically mapped; indeed, many experts claim it to be the finest ring dyke in the British Isles. The Ring occurred as a result of volcanic activity that convulsed this area around sixty million years ago, hence the 16km-wide circle of craggy mini-mountains you see today. Topping the lot is Slieve Gullion (573m), a mysteriously beautiful mountain rich in romantic legends, not least that concerning Cúchulainn (pronounced cooh-Cullen) - the hero of the *Táin Bó Cúailnge* (Cattle Raid of Cooley), who took his name here after slaying the hound (*Cú*) of the blacksmith Culainn. It's a short, sharp trek to the top, and worth it for the superlative and memorable outlook, both of the north and south of Ireland.

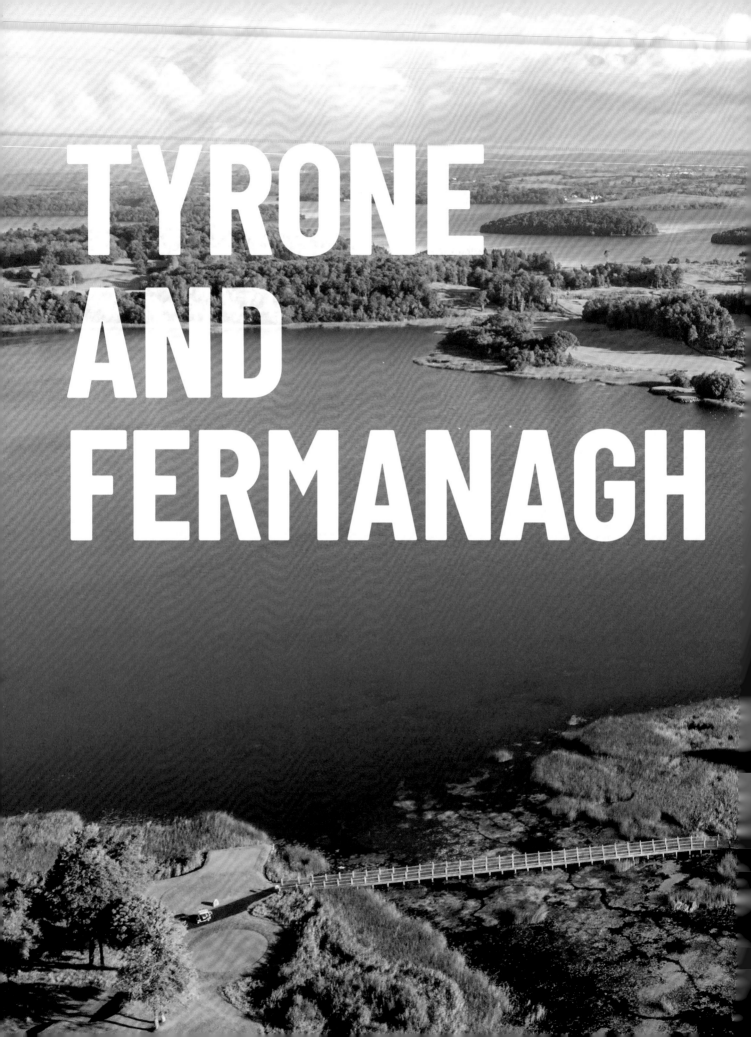

TYRONE AND FERMANAGH

A long route ahead

Mountain sheep

One of the many routes

Vast walking tracks

Appropriate hiking gear is essential

THE SPERRINS

It is the largest mountain range in Northern Ireland, yet The Sperrins are in many ways forgotten – and that's just the way the locals like it. A succession of whaleback peaks, the highest of which is Sawel at 678m, The Sperrins get their name from the Irish Na Speirini, meaning 'spurs of rock', though they are much smoother and more rounded than this implies. They date back 600 million years and comprise low-grade slate, and quartz, which is the source of the local tradition of panning for gold. Indeed, tales abound concerning the discovery of "gold in them thar hills", and you might still encounter the occasio-

nal panner testing the story's veracity. But don't get ahead of yourself: even if you panned for a year, you'd do well to find enough for a small filling. With vast tracks of hills, mile upon mile of bog and heather, and very little else for a long, long way, this is walking country par excellence: if you want to go the whole hog, the Central Sperrins Way is a fantastic 40km waymarked trail along the spine of the range, beginning at Gortin and ending in Moneyneany.

The rustic buildings in the park

ULSTER AMERICAN FOLK PARK

Of all of Northern Ireland's American-heritage projects, the wonderful Ulster American Folk Park is by far the most rewarding. Set within some thirty acres of rolling countryside a few miles northwest of Omagh in County Tyrone, the park recalls how, during the eighteenth and nineteenth centuries, more than two million Ulster people left their homes to forge a new life across the Atlantic. Rich in originality, it's brought colourfully to life by an array of costumed characters going about their everyday lives among the shops and thatched cottages in the Old World and the log cabins and plantation houses of the New. Transporting you between the Old (Ulster) and the New (America) Worlds is a full-replica early 1800s ship, aboard which you'll 'experience' a tiny slither of the long and gruelling crossing across the North Atlantic. Try and coincide a visit with the rip-roaring Bluegrass Festival in early September, which invariably plays host to a stellar cast of musicians.

Storytelling at the park

Performers at Bluegrass Festival

A farrier hammering out horseshoes in the forge

The 'Old World'

Enniskillen Castle

Enjoying a pint in *Blake's* pub

Lough Erne

The pub's inviting exterior

ENNISKILLEN

A cheerful little market town framed by two narrow ribbons of water connecting the Lower and Upper sections of Lough Erne, Enniskillen happily lays claim to being Northern Ireland's only island town. Contained within its delightful streetscape, a few must-sees include Headhunters, a barber's shop-cum-railway museum (yes, really); the Buttermarket, a nineteenth-century stone dairy market now home to resident craftsfolk; and the enduringly popular *Blakes of the Hollow*, once described by the Irish writer Colm Tóibín as 'a cathedral of a pub'. Go see for yourself. From Enniskillen it's a short way to Lough Erne, two connected lakes that epitomise Fermanagh's profoundly important relationship with water: indeed, an old adage maintains that for six months Lough Erne is in Fermanagh, and for the rest of the year Fermanagh is in Lough Erne. It's all very much *Swallows and Amazons* territory: boats, fishing, uninhabited islands and monastic ruins, ripe for endless exploration, whatever your age.

The bubble domes are perfect for stargazing

Gourmet dining is the order of the day in *The Barn*

One of the lovely lake houses

The outdoor hot tub

FINN LOUGH

Bubble domes to sleep under the stars, split-level lake houses with the dreamiest views, and a restaurant with a tasting menu that is out of this world, Finn Lough delivers with finesse. Nestled quietly on a sheltered stretch of Lough Erne, with views of Boa Island across the water, this innovative getaway sits on a little peninsula in Enniskillen, Fermanagh. An adults-only oasis of peace, this is the place to come for superb service, a serene lakeside setting and restorative spa treatments. Follow the Elements spa nature trail along the edge of the lake to luxuriate in the heated saltwater floatation pool followed by the Finnish sauna, before a cooling plunge in the lake; then onto the aromatherapy sauna, hot tub and relaxation room. Emerge renewed in mind, body and soul. Cycle or walk the woodland paths, watch a film in the plush cinema, luxuriate in the breakfast hamper delivered to your door, grab a lazy lunch in the bar and be blown away by the fine dining in *The Barn* at night.

The sauna with its lake views

Rock formations

The minecarts

Stalactites formed over hundreds of years

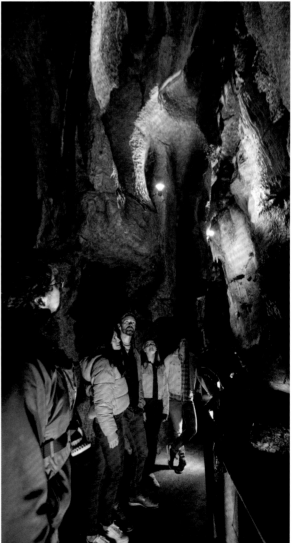

A guided tour explains all the different formations

MARBLE ARCH CAVES

There is something inherently fascinating about the subterranean world, and so it is with the Marble Arch Caves, which were first discovered in 1895 by Frenchman Edouard Martel and Dublin zoologist Henry Lyster Jameson, although they weren't revealed to the public until 1985. Following a pleasant little walk down through the reserve, the guided tour begins with a short boat journey along the underground Cladagh River, before continuing on *terra firma* through a succession of lofty chambers and tightly wound passages. Throughout, clusters of weirdly shaped stalactites and stalagmites, as well as other impressive formations such as flowstones and scallops (sculpted indentations caused by water flow) constantly vie for your attention. As is standard practice in the world of show caves, many of these formations have been assigned peculiar names, like Porridge Pot and Guardian Angel, although it does occasionally require a degree of lateral thinking to understand why.

STAIRWAY TO HEAVEN

A wonderful hike seemingly into the heavens, this walk demands a certain level of fitness in order to ascend the steep incline, but the arrival at the top is reward enough. Covering the biggest expanse of blanket bog in Ireland, the Stairway to Heaven walk, also known as the Cuilcagh Boardwalk Trail, takes you over gravel tracks, boardwalk and, you guessed it, steps. The route is just under 15km-long and is rated as difficult, mainly due to the gradual incline and the 1.5km-long steep staircase. Expect it to take around four hours to complete. It's located in the UNESCO Marble Arch Geopark, a special conservation area. Along the route, enjoy views of the protected bogland around you and the natural flora and fauna endemic to the area. At the top, stop for a breather and soak in the views before a more leisurely return back down to earth.

INDEX

CONTRIBUTORS

Siobhan Canavan

George Keegan

Mundy Walsh

Kate Drynan

Norm Longley

Allanah Hopkin

Niall O'Donaghue

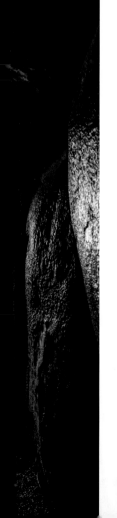

PHOTO CREDITS